4050

W9-BDA-382

The Directors Guild of America Oral History Series

1. Byron Haskin. 1984.
2. Worthington Miner. 1985.
3. Curtis Bernhardt. 1986.
4. King Vidor. 1988.
5. David Butler.
6. Stuart Heisler.
7. Henry Koster. 1987.
8. Ira Skutch. 1989.
9. Norman Lloyd. 1990.
10. Jack, Jules, & Sam White. 1990.
11. Arthur Jacobson. 1991.

A Directors Guild of America Oral History

ARTHUR JACOBSON

Interviewed by
Irene Kahn Atkins

The Directors Guild of America &
The Scarecrow Press, Inc.
Metuchen, N.J., & London, 1991

British Library Cataloguing-in-Publication data available

Library of Congress Cataloging-in-Publication data

Jacobson, Arthur, 1901-
Arthur Jacobson / interviewed by Irene Kahn Atkins.
p. cm. -- (The Directors Guild of America oral history series ; 11)
Includes index.
ISBN 0-8108-2468-X (alk. paper)
1. Jacobson, Arthur, 1901- --Interviews. 2. Motion picture producers and directors--United States--Interviews. I. Atkins, Irene Kahn, 1922- . II. Title. III. Series: Directors Guild of America oral history ; 11.
PN1998.3.J27A3 1991
791.43'0233'092--dc20 91-27516

Manufactured in the United States of America
Printed on acid-free paper

To Toni — all my love

Table of Contents

Foreword and Acknowledgments

Arthur Jacobson, whose career in the film industry spanned six technological and innovative decades, began as a cameraman when the job required you to own your own camera. Artie witnessed and participated in the transitions from silents to sound, black-and-white to color, and Academy aperture to widescreen formats. In telling his story he sheds light on many stars, directors, and films of the silent and sound era. He worked with Clara Bow in both New York and Hollywood on such films as *The Saturday Night Kid, The Wild Party,* and *No Limit.* He was assistant director to some of the most outstanding directors in film — Frank Borzage, Henry King, Josef von Sternberg, William Wellman, Dorothy Arzner, George Cukor, Wesley Ruggles, and George Seaton. Valued for his special ability to solve all the logistical problems on the sets of Hollywood productions, Artie worked on a number of films which are part of American cultural history: *An American Tragedy, Miracle on 34th Street, I Was a Male War Bride,* and *The Bridges of Toko-Ri.*

There are many people to thank for this book. First and foremost is Arthur Jacobson himself for becoming part of the Guild's ongoing oral history series. During the final editing phase of this manuscript, I met with Artie and he retold some of the stories included in this book. Hearing him tell them in his own voice was to hear the excitement he had for this art form. We are lucky indeed that he was able to share his experiences with us.

David Shepard, DGA Special Projects Officer from 1976 - 1987, developed the Guild's oral history program as part of an ongoing series to document past achievements in film, television and radio. He oversaw this oral history from its inception through the archival transcript stage. Unfortunately, Irene Atkins, who interviewed Artie, passed away shortly after completing the interviews. Additional transcribing, researching, and editing assistance was provided by Adele Field, Nick Lovrovich, Ira Skutch, W. Richard Ackerman, Deac Rossell, Laraine Savelle, and David Stenn.

Selise E. Eiseman
National Special Projects Officer
January 1991

Introduction

When I began my biography of Clara Bow, a wise man at the Directors Guild named David Shepard suggested I meet Arthur Jacobson. The name was not familiar to me, but of course I called anyway — and as a result, I found an invaluable source and supportive friend.

I was all ears for "Artie," and my attention was repaid with one incredible, true tale after another, all told by a man with an astoundingly accurate memory ("I was there, Charlie," he would warn me when I dared doubt a detail — and invariably he was right) and a love for his craft which, as he approaches age ninety, remains in full enthusiastic force.

Clara Bow: Runnin' Wild allowed me to meet many veterans of the movie industry, most of whom shared their memories with grace and charm. None of them, however, had anything on Artie. His own experience was so rich and full that I was soon wondering why it had not been recorded.

Now that situation has been rectified, and we are all the more fortunate for it. Artie Jacobson was indeed there, Charlie — and the oral history preserved here is a fascinating, fitting testament to his presence.

David Stenn

The Studios of New York

IRENE KAHN ATKINS: When were you born? And where?

ARTHUR JACOBSON: In New York City, on October 23, 1901.

ATKINS: Tell me about your family. Were they in show business?

JACOBSON: Absolutely not. My father was in the embroidery business. I went to high school around the corner from the Biograph Studios. They had a big glass roof over it, and every night it was lit with a blue light, which aroused my curiosity. I found out what was going on: they were making motion pictures. So I snuck in one night, like any New York kid would, saw all the beautiful dames around, and said, "This is for me."

ATKINS: How old were you then?

JACOBSON: Oh, about sixteen. I found out who the head of one of the departments was. I didn't even know what they did in that department. I waited for him, and approached him with a typical New York kid's chutzpah. I asked him for a job during the summer vacation.

He asked me what I could do, and I said I could work. He asked me if I was experienced at anything. I said,

"Just work. I'll do anything you want me to do, but I want to work in the studio."

He said, "I can't use you. You're too young, to start with, and you know nothing."

I decided that I was going to get a job in that studio, and I had the determination to do it. I lived around the corner and every morning of the ten weeks that I was off on summer vacation I would say, "Good morning," to him. When he went to lunch, came back from lunch, and when he went home, there I was. His name was Palmer, and he turned out to be the head of the electrical department.

Before the ten weeks were up he capitulated and gave me a job cleaning lamps. I was paid seven dollars a week, but the overtime was such that I was getting in the neighborhood of twelve and fourteen, because they worked every night. I fell in love with the business.

ATKINS: Were you also interested in going to the movies?

JACOBSON: Oh, sure. I remember one time as a kid, that the leading lady of the picture came and made a personal appearance. I fell in love with her. Her name was Lillian Walker.

In sitting up on top of the set with a spotlight, I could look down and see who did what. I found out that the director was the head man, so I decided right there and then that I was going to become a director. But in the next few weeks I realized that the director's mind could be changed by the cameraman. I said, "The hell with that. I'm going to become a cameraman."

I took the few bucks that I had, and went to the New York Institute of Photography and learned how to be a photographer. I was a hack, but I knew how to focus, and my pictures came out.

ATKINS: Was it a legitimate school?

JACOBSON: Oh, yes. It was advertised in all the magazines. When it came to studying the motion picture camera I quit because I didn't want to spend any more money. I could learn during the lunch hour, by playing around with the camera if they didn't see me. I got in trouble a couple of times, because a dissolve was in the camera, and I screwed that up.

I worked so hard and so long, my father came to the studio at about two a.m. one morning, and said, "Get out of here. Your mother's home crying because you're working with all these tramps." The movie women wore their makeup very thick.

He dragged me out of the studio and I had a hell of a time getting back, because the head of the department didn't want to get mixed up with my parents. I went to work for my father, but eventually I got back in the studio. Only this time I became an assistant cameraman.

ATKINS: Had you quit school?

JACOBSON: Oh, sure. The hell with school. I only went to high school for six months. I wound up in the studio, and was there for a few years. I worked on every picture that was made at the studio. I was an electrician, a handyman, a gofer, anything.

I did a picture with the original Dolly Sisters called *Million Dollar Dollies* in 1918. In 1945, I was assigned as an assistant director to *The Dolly Sisters*, with Betty Grable and June Haver. George Jessel was the producer.

I came on the picture after someone else had been taken off, and after working the first day, I went to George's office and said, "George, I don't know whether you know it or not, but you're making a big mistake. I worked with the Dolly Sisters. They were both black-haired Hungarians. You've got Betty and June — blondes."

All George said to me was, "S-h-h-h-h." So I shushed.

ATKINS: Can you tell me a little more about the Biograph Studios?

JACOBSON: Well, it was a rental studio. They rented out space to various people, and it was nothing like the studios we eventually had in Hollywood. It was a combination of two buildings. One building was three stories high, with this great glass roof over it.

ATKINS: That was the one you saw the blue light through? What sort of light was it?

JACOBSON: It was called a Cooper-Hewitt. It was a long tubular light, and it was blue, very much like neon lights. Every once in a while one of them would start to flicker out, and you had to take it out and change it. Each light had a reflector over it, and they had what they called banks of lights, six or eight of them in one spot. They had goosenecks that could change the direction of the light.

One of my first jobs was to get up on a ladder and clean all the reflectors. You didn't have to know anything. It was just a matter of having a rag and cleaning them. If you weren't careful, you got an electric shock and fell off the ladder. The boys knew that. As a new boy, I fell on my royal American arse many times. They thought it was funny, so I laughed. I got to be pals with them, and that was very nice.

The studio, per se, had one lower stage and one upper stage. The other building was a laboratory, where you took the film for developing and printing during the night.

They also had a little department where you developed and printed still pictures. They had their own camera. Once I became an assistant cameraman, I was also the still man. After the regular day's work was over, I used to work all night long, developing and printing the stills at a nickel each. If there were twenty stills I'd get a dollar. It was good money.

ATKINS: Did they have several companies shooting on the various stages?

JACOBSON: Oh, yes, absolutely. Back to back. Many times a cameraman would have to move his camera a little bit, because the guy who was shooting another picture was in his way.

We also had two cameras on every picture. We had one camera, the main camera, which was for the American negative. The other one was used for the foreign negative, because they made a lot of money in Europe.

ATKINS: Why did they need a different kind of a negative?

JACOBSON: The main negative was where their money was. They didn't want to take a chance on sending the negative to Europe, and having prints made. The laws were very strange. If you printed them over there it was cheaper. There were so many ramifications.

ATKINS: They didn't just make dupe negatives?

JACOBSON: No. They could have, but it would have been too expensive.

ATKINS: How many companies would they have shooting at one time at the Biograph Studio?

JACOBSON: They only had two on the lower stage. On the upper stage, there were sometimes three. They were small stages, but they were small pictures, also.

I can't think of anything else about Biograph except to describe the place itself. You entered an ordinary looking building. I think it was at 807 - 175th Street, between Marmion and Clinton Avenues. That's in the Upper Bronx. There was a commissary on the second floor. I don't think it ever won a blue ribbon. They had all the things that were necessary. They made movies.

ATKINS: Who owned the studio at that time?

JACOBSON: I don't know who actually owned the studio, but a man named Tom Persons was the studio manager.

At the Biograph Studio, we made a picture with a great comedian and comedienne, a team called Charlie Murray and Kate Price. Ray Rockett was the producer. He was the brother of Al Rockett, a big First National producer.

We were going to shoot on location, on a boat. We got together about six o'clock one morning, went to City Island by automobile, and got on the boat. We couldn't work off City Island because it was too smooth. They wanted the boat to rock. We took the boat clear down to Far Rockaway, which was a long ways.

I went down to the cabin to get Kate Price. I must have been the assistant director, because that would have been part of my job. There she was, in tears. I asked her, "What's the matter?"

She said she just realized that she had left her false teeth in the studio, in a glass in her dressing room. There was nothing much we could do.

There was one scene where the leading man, whose name I can't remember, had to jump overboard and swim. Even though we were near to shore, he was scared to death. The director said, "We have to get somebody else to jump in. Anybody to do it? Twenty-five bucks."

I volunteered, I put the actor's clothes on, and jumped in. I came back, but I never got the twenty-five dollars.

They did another picture, *Lest We Forget*. It was about the sinking of the Lusitania. They built a piece of the bow, as the thing was sinking. You saw the bow sticking up in the air, and it was shot against the sky so you couldn't tell it was on land. They built it on some backlot about ten miles from the studio, and charged the public twenty-five cents a head to watch us shoot.

ATKINS: Like the Universal Studios tour.

JACOBSON: Exactly. The star of the film was Rita Jolivet. The director was Leonce Perret. The cameraman was French. The camera itself was French. We had two famous leading men who played in *Million Dollar Dollies*: Bradley Barker and Huntley Gordon.

While I was at Biograph, my great ambition was to work at Paramount on Long Island. I did get that opportunity soon after, but just before moving over there, I had a wonderful experience.

We did a thing up on the Hudson River, with the Denis-Shawn Dancers — the great Ted Shawn and Ruth St. Denis company with all their dancing girls. We were shooting along a stone wall, and they were dancing toward me. As luck would have it, just as they reached the gate in the stone wall, a wind gust hit it and the gate swung open. The lead girl danced through it for no reason at all. It was never rehearsed, but the other girls followed her. My boss thought this was a great piece of artistic work.

ATKINS: It seems that in the silent days there were many shorts and features that called for music, but had no music furnished for the film. How did they shoot that? Did they have somebody playing the piano?

JACOBSON: I can't remember. But we had lots of offstage music in the silents, for mood. If it was a big company we had three pieces; a little company, two pieces. We always had a little portable organ and a violin, and if it was a big picture which had a third piece, we used a viola.

When Gloria Swanson, for instance, was going to do an emotional scene, and they wanted four cuts, they didn't do it with one camera and take it four times at different angles. They used four cameras, and off to the side were the musicians.

There was a strange thing about that music, because as a cameraman you didn't have electrically driven cameras. You had to crank by hand, so many frames to the second, so many frames to the minute, so to speak. If you slowed down, the images on the screen would be going fast, like a comedy. If you went fast, it would be like slow motion. So you always had to be steady. If you got carried away by the music and what you were watching, you could very easily slow down without realizing it. You had to see the images, and close your ears to the music.

Nowadays, the finders that you look through are very big, but we had one that was only the size of the frame. You had to pan and tilt the camera by hand, and all the time you were cranking. When you'd get a shot where a man was coming down the stairs, you brought him down with the tilt. When he got to the bottom of the stairs and started to walk across the room, you had to move over, pan the camera, and, at the same time, crank at the regular speed. If he changed his mind and went back up the stairs, you had to do the whole thing again, in reverse.

But, like Fred Astaire said, you had to keep practicing all the time. I couldn't practice with an empty camera, so

I'd have about four hundred feet of lead film, and when I wasn't working, I'd carry my camera with me and practice with that.

There was a thing called a pressure plate inside the camera. You had to be careful that the emulsion on the film didn't get scratched from the pressure plate. After every scene, you always took it out and goose-greased it. Even today, no scene is complete until the assistant cameraman has taken the plate out and examined it. If there's the slightest scratch, he says, "Butterfly," which means you have to do the whole thing all over again.

When we made a scene with Technicolor, if anything went wrong with the film, they gave you another roll of film. Sometimes you spent $100,000 on one scene, and if something was wrong, they gave you another roll of film. Ever since pictures started, it's been an expensive risk to make movies.

ATKINS: When did they start using motor-driven cameras?

JACOBSON: I don't remember. It was a calamity when they went from the Bell and Howell to the Mitchell camera. On a Bell and Howell, you had three lenses. You racked it over, and got in position after you lined it all up. It was beautiful because it was all ball bearings.

With the Mitchell camera, you racked it in the opposite direction. On the first day we ever worked with it the cameraman forgot to rack it over. The laboratory called the cameraman in the middle of the night and said, "There's nothing on your film."

It was not in photographing position. Fortunately, all the film in my camera, the second camera, was okay. We went down there in a hurry, did a little conniving, and cut the slates off one and put it on the other. Then we had a dupe made, so we had two negatives. The company never did know it.

ATKINS: You worked on *Zaza* at the Astoria Studios in 1923.

JACOBSON: Yes. They had four cameras, and music on the side. Going out there meant going by subway and waiting and waiting. I finally got a job as the third assistant cameraman on *Zaza*, but I was just a camera gofer.

Anyhow, I got through that, and now I was working at Paramount as the third assistant cameraman. Henry Cronjager was the cameraman. He was a big, tall man.

Irvin Willat, the director, dressed very nautically. Of course, many directors dressed the part for the kind of story they were making. He had been a cameraman, and invented a "seagoing tripod," to get the rocking and pitching effect of shooting in a boat. A piece of metal attached to a bowling ball with a nail in it was hung from the camera tripod. The numeral 8 was written on the floor. I sat on the floor with the bowling ball and traced the number 8 with the nail, which gave the camera the effect of rolling and pitching.

Irvin Willat was mean to people — not to me, but to others. They were doing a scene with the star, Madge Kennedy, while the musicians played. All of a sudden he said, "Cut!," looked over at the violinist and said, "Why don't you learn to play that goddamn thing? You hit a flat note, for Christ's sake. Don't ever do that again."

All the time he was talking, he was twirling his little megaphone around his wrist, and all of a sudden he let it fly, and he hit the guy on the back of his ear with the megaphone.

I thought to myself, what would I do if he did anything like that to me? I wouldn't take it the way this man did. When we got through that night, I went to Mr. Gaine, the studio manager who had given me the job, and quit. He asked me why, and I told him. He said, "You'll get used to things like that." I said I never would, but he said he'd put me on another picture, which he did. Incidentally, that picture was *Three Miles Out*.

ATKINS: What was the Astoria Studio like, physically, in 1923?

JACOBSON: Oh, it was the Taj Mahal of motion picture making. Don't forget, I had never been to Hollywood. I had never seen a big studio. The only studios I worked in were around New York, and they were all little shacks that had been made into studios.

I sponged around for jobs, and the fact that I had a camera got me a lot of jobs, because most of the cameramen had their cameras in hock.

I did some comedies with a director who became big at MGM, Richard Thorpe. We worked out on Long Island, Glendale, which meant that I had to take my camera out of my house in the morning, get on the subway, go down to the Pennsylvania Station, get on the Long Island Railroad, and go to the studio. I got the same salary, but I was almost bent over carrying the camera and the tripod.

I've got to tell you a story about Marion Davies. William Randolph Hearst set up Cosmopolitan Productions, and he built a two-level studio in Harlem, right on the Harlem River, at 127th Street and Second Avenue. It was tremendous. There was room for two companies. They would rent out space to another company when it was necessary.

Hearst proceeded to make some of the biggest pictures in the business. He knew nothing about the motion picture business, but he hired the finest people, cameramen, writers, directors. He was going to make a star out of Marion Davies or bust! There used to be full page ads in all the Hearst papers. Although she was very clever, very funny and a very beautiful dame, he never succeeded in making a great star out of her.

Marion Davies' dressing room was at the top, which meant she had to walk up a flight of stairs. She complained about that one time, so a whole construction crew came in, knocked the walls down, and put in an elevator.

I was working for *The Federated Screen Revue,* which was in competition with *Screen Snapshots* — two or three subjects on a 15-minute reel. They were about the stars and how they lived at home, and it was part of my job to try to get the subjects.

One day my boss said to me, "Gosh, if we could just get Marion Davies, we could devote the whole reel to her. If you can get her, I'll give you a twenty-five dollar raise.

Twenty-five dollars was a bloody fortune! I went up to the studio and said to somebody, "How do you get to talk to Marion Davies?"

He said, "You must be kidding. Nobody talks to Marion Davies."

The cameraman was named Ira Morgan, and Marion never made a bit of film unless he photographed it. There was a second cameraman who was also part of her group. You could get to Marion Davies through her secretary, who was going with the second cameraman. I put two and two together, and got acquainted with him, on my way in and out of the studio. I found out that he drank, and where he had his drinks. I met him at the bar a couple of times and bought him a couple of drinks. It didn't take long until we became buddy-buddy. I told him what I wanted to do, knowing that he and the secretary were buddy-buddy. Finally he introduced me to Williams — her name was just one word. I told Williams what I wanted to do. She said that I could do it, but that Ira Morgan would have to photograph it.

I was taken in and introduced to Miss Davies. Much to my embarrassment, and I don't embarrass easily, when she started to talk to me, she stuttered. And freckles! I can see all the freckles. But everything was fine. I was to come to the studio Monday morning, all prepared. I could bring my camera, but I couldn't use it.

We went up to the stage. I thought we were all going to meet and go to her home, but no — they had built a set, with a living room, bedroom and a kitchen. It was all lit, just like a regular set. They had costumed her. Her hair was fixed. She came down, and we worked all day doing this. Then I was told to come back the next night and see the rushes with them, which I did. They supplied a cutter, and they cut the film the way I wanted it. They looked at the finished film and everybody was happy. They signed the releases and kissed me goodbye.

There I was, with the film and a twenty-five dollar raise staring me in the face. I went to my boss, whose name was Arthur D. V. Storey. He drank, and smoked stogies which stank. I told him the whole story of getting the film. He gave me the money for the film that was used, and he gave me the twenty-five dollar raise. That was the first raise I ever got in the motion picture business.

ATKINS: Do you think any of the *Federated Screen Revues* are still extant?

JACOBSON: I don't know. Arthur Storey, the producer, had been the cutter for *Screen Snapshots,* which were made by CBC Film Sales — Cohn, Brandt, and Cohn. One of the two Cohns was Harry Cohn. Storey had an argument with them and they fired him. So he set up his own company in competition with them, and hired me as the cameraman, because I had a camera.

The first feature pictures I worked on as a cameraman were *Puritan Passions, The Scarecrow,* and *Grit.*

The Scarecrow was directed by Frank Tuttle and starred Glenn Hunter and Mary Astor.

Grit was an independent picture with Glenn Hunter and Clara Bow, directed by Frank Tuttle. The producer was Ray Smallwood.

They had rented a little studio across from the 92nd Street ferryboat. When everybody went in to see the first day's rushes, with Frank Tuttle, the film was trembling on the screen. We went back and examined the cameras every which way. We examined the tripods and the tripod heads. We couldn't find anything. The next morning when we started to work, we could hear a rumble. The studio was so old that when you were grinding the camera, the floor that the tripod was on would shake. That's how broken-down those studios were.

Off to Hollywood

JACOBSON: A result of the picture *Grit* was that I fell in love. I was nineteen or twenty. I fell in love with a girl who was three years my junior, named Clara Bow. At night, I used to go all the way out to Brooklyn, where she lived, and take her to Chinese restaurants. She lived at 44 Church Street, in a brownstone, and we used to sit on the top of the stoop and make love, so to speak. She was dynamite. She was a pistol.

Before the picture was over, a man named Jack Bachman came and offered her a contract for Hollywood. He was the eastern representative of B. P. Schulberg, who was a big shot out there. He offered her two hundred bucks a week. When she went to Hollywood, I waited five days, and I couldn't stand it any longer. I drew out my savings — eight hundred dollars — and went to Hollywood to see her. I got a room right off Hollywood Boulevard and Kingsley Drive. I think I paid five bucks a week for it.

Clara didn't know where the hell she was, there was so much going on. First she lived in a hotel and then she moved to a house. Her father came out. He was nuts, but he trusted me, the damn fool. It didn't take long before they insisted that I move out of that room and move in with them. The house had three bedrooms. I offered to pay part of the rent, but they had a housekeeper, and we arranged that I would pay her salary.

When I was working for Schulberg, he called me in one day, and asked, "Where do you live?"

I told him, and he said, "You're the man we've been looking for. You're living with Clara Bow."

I said, "I'm living in the house with her and her father."

He said, "You're living with my big star. Now you get the hell out of that house, or there's going to be a scandal." He fired me.

When she came home that night, I said, "I'm moving."

She asked why, and I told her. The next morning she went in and tore up her contract and threw it in his face, and told him he couldn't run her private life.

ATKINS: Aside from the fact that you were in love with her, what was she like?

JACOBSON: Oh, just great. As an actress, she was great. She was fine until sound came in. She was what we called a free-wheeling actress. She didn't have any lines to study. The cameramen they put on her pictures got used to her. They knew how to light and how to follow with the camera, because once she started to play a scene you never knew where she was going to be. No director wanted to hold her down. They let her go! A couple of times they had to say, "Well, you can't do that, because we're photographing the studio."

ATKINS: Did they use three or four cameras with her?

JACOBSON: If it was necessary. She never insisted upon anything. No music, none of that junk. "Just tell me what I have to do and I'll do it." She was a ball. As I said, I worked on very few pictures with her, but we were great friends. By that time, she'd been having affairs with everybody, including Gary Cooper. I was going with a girl whom I eventually married, and she and Clara became great friends. Clara fell in love with one of the kids working in a picture named Rex Bell. He played the sailor in *True to the Navy*.

Clara did strange things. We were working on *The Saturday Night Kid*. Someone brought two koalas on the set. She bought them right there, and took them home. They made a mess, and she couldn't find any help. At the other house, on Hollywood Boulevard, which still stands, someone told her that she shouldn't leave her two dogs in the backyard. She brought the dogs into the spare bedroom, and had someone cover the floor of the room with dirt. When she sold the house, she had to replace the floor.

Clara had some trouble breathing. The doctor, Wesley Hommel, said that they would have to operate on her nose some day, and that it would take three or four weeks to heal.

Colleen Moore's husband was a producer at First National Pictures, which is now Paramount Studios. Clara was given the second lead to Colleen Moore in a picture. Frank Lloyd was the director, and Billy Tummell was the assistant.

One night, Clara came home and she was really steaming. She rarely got mad, but she called Colleen everything under the sun. It seems that after a certain scene was shot and they had made all of the closeups of Colleen Moore, the director wanted to turn around and make closeups of Clara. Colleen Moore objected. She said she didn't think it was necessary to have closeups of Clara.

Clara said, "I'll get that girl," or something like that. In those days women didn't use the kind of language they use today. I'm sure, however, that she said, "that bitch," or something to that effect. Clara didn't have to work the next day, so she kept on steaming.

In the meantime, at the studio, they had struck the entire set, because it was a rental deal, and they only had one stage. The scene in which Colleen wouldn't let her do her closeup had hundreds of extras. It was a very expensive proposition, and now it was all on film. The following day, the new set was there, Clara got her call, and she said, "I'm not going to go back to work. I'm sick. I'll get back at her. I know it's her own company but — ."

I said, "Clara, you've got to go to work. You can't do that in this business."

She said, "Watch me. I'm not mad at the business. I'm not mad at anybody, but she had no right to kill those closeups that they were going to make of me. I'm going to take a walk."

She took a walk, and she didn't come back home for four or five hours. We got a little worried. She had a call for the next day. At ten o'clock that night she walked in. She was bandaged from chin to forehead. I asked her if she'd been in an accident.

She said, "No. But remember my nose had to be operated on? Remember, Wesley said any time I wanted it done I didn't even have to go to a hospital. I had it done in his office this afternoon."

"In the middle of a picture? Are you crazy?"

Her father spoke up and said, "If that's what my baby wants, that's what my baby does."

She never notified anybody. The next morning the phone rang, and it was Billy Tummell. I told him he'd better come over and talk to her. He came over, walked in the bedroom and saw her. Then the director and the producer came over. They had to rebuild the sets, put all the extras back in, and recast the picture. She was taken off, because they couldn't wait three weeks for her to heal. They gave the part to a woman named Violet Mersereau. That's the way Clara was. She was the sweetest girl in the world, but you didn't cross her and you didn't do her wrong.

I was on a talking picture with Clara called *Kick In,* which Richard Wallace directed. She had to stay home and study words. She had to play a scene and read lines. She just couldn't go running all over the place. It was like putting a straitjacket on her. She had one enemy on the set, the microphone. She got to a point where she'd start to play a scene, and as she was playing the scene, she would look at the enemy, which was hanging up above the camera. She didn't know she was doing it. Dick Wallace, who was the finest director in the world, and such a wonderful guy, tried to explain to her that she couldn't do that.

One day she just went berserk. She couldn't get the words or the scene right. No drink, nothing like that, just sound. There were too many people telling her, "You can't do it this way, you can't do it that way." She reached up, right in the middle of the scene, and hit the microphone with her fist and said, "You son-of-a-bitch," and then went berserk, completely hysterical. They had to take her to her dressing room.

I took her home. We had a hell of a time finishing that picture. They put things around so you couldn't see the microphones. They put them in chandeliers or something. Otherwise her eyes kept going to it. Anyhow, when that was over there was no more career.

One night, she invited us all to dinner at her home in Beverly Hills, at 512 North Bedford Drive. At the end of dinner Rex said, "I've got an announcement to make to all of Clara's friends. Your friendships are all over as of this moment. She loves you all. You love her, but the only way to keep her sanity is to get her out of this business, and get her out of this town, no more Hollywood."

At that time Rex had a ranch up at Searchlight, Nevada. He also had a store in Las Vegas, a tack store, with jodhpurs and saddles. He took her out of Hollywood, sold the house, and took her to Searchlight.

That was the last we ever saw of her, up to a given point. She was looking for something to do, so she learned to ride horseback. They tell me that they had to take the horses away from her. She ran them into the ground. She was so full of energy.

We went to Las Vegas some time later, and I ran into Rex in the lobby of the hotel. I asked how Clara was. He said, "All right."

I said, "Will you please come down and have dinner with me?" He refused.

"Why?"

"What I told you that night still goes."

I said, "Can we come out and see you?"

"No, no."

I asked, "Does she know this?"

"Yes," he said, "but I'll tell her that I did see you."

About a year later, I got a call, and she was seven-and-a-half months pregnant. We were asked to come and visit with her at Rex's mother's home, a little place on Swall Drive. We went up. If I hadn't heard her talk, I wouldn't have known it was Clara Bow. She must have weighed a hundred and eighty pounds. The only thing you could recognize was the red hair and the stutter. That was part of her charm.

She had made Rex set up a 16-millimeter screen, and she had all these books of her pictures, and all the home movies they had made. We spent the saddest evening, and that's the last time I ever saw Clara.

Next, I heard that she had become very ill. By this time she'd had two more children — and had lost her mind. I didn't believe that. Finally I heard that she was in a sanitarium on Overland Avenue, and I went there. I never got beyond the woman who took care of her. I said to her, "Please give her my address, my phone number."

Christmas came and we got a Christmas card, and inside the card, in childish writing, was everything she'd done during the whole year. I found out that she sent six of those every year: one to Louella Parsons, one to Hedda Hopper, one to us and to three other friends. This went on for about ten years, and the next thing I knew she had died. Rex had become lieutenant-governor of Nevada. I went to the funeral, after I had given it a great deal of thought. I wanted to remember her the way I knew her — the fun we had. I went, and there was an open casket. I looked at a complete stranger. A woman lay there in that casket, who I had never seen in my life. That was the end of Clara Bow. It was very sad.

When I first got to California, I had my own camera, but I couldn't get a job, because I was from the East, and the union wouldn't let me in. So I worked on anything I could. Then I went back to New York by way of the Panama Canal, worked on a few things there, and then returned to Hollywood. This time I was allowed to do some extra camera work because they didn't have the men to fill certain jobs that came up.

ATKINS: Do you remember the names of any of those films?

JACOBSON: No. They were one, two, three day jobs. The big one was at Paramount, starring Pola Negri. Herbert Brenon was the director. Arthur Grant, the head of the camera department, sent word out that anybody who could find an Akeley camera was to come and work at the studio for two days, at seventy-five dollars a day. I knew a man at FBO Studios, which became RKO, who owned an Akeley camera. I didn't know how to work it, but for seventy-five bucks a day I'd learn. I tried to borrow it, but he was in Europe.

One of the pictures I had done in New York was with a dog called Strongheart. It was a little episode in *Screen Snapshots*. The dog's producer had an Akeley camera. I found out where he was, went to him, and begged and pleaded. He said, "I'll let you use the camera on one condition: that you take my cameraman with you. I don't want anybody to fuss with the camera except John Leezer.

You'll have to pay him the going rate." The going rate at that time was thirty-five dollars a day.

I called Grant, and he hired me. I got hold of Leezer, and went to the studio, which in those days was the Famous Players Studio, on Vine Street. I can't remember the name of the picture. The leading man was French. The big scene was when the couple danced. They wanted a big close two-shot. So they had to have a special camera for it.

ATKINS: What was so special about it?

JACOBSON: It was the first time they did a dance scene in closeup. I borrowed Clara's car, picked up the camera and the cameraman, went to Paramount, and became his assistant. I just carried the camera around. But at the end of each day I got seventy-five bucks, thirty-five for him, and forty for me.

I figured it as a one or two day job, but Ray Lissner was the assistant director, and he and Pola got along fine. Ray winked at me, and when five o'clock rolled around, he said, "Pola, you don't want to do that difficult dance shot today, do you?"

She said, "Oh, Ray, darling, tomorrow."

I worked for five days. He did it for me. In the five days I made two hundred dollars. That weekend I took the whole gang down to the Cocoanut Grove at the Ambassador Hotel and spent the two hundred dollars. I was a young man.

Here's the way they used to make pictures at RKO. When Schulberg and Jaffe were independent producers there, Charles Lang and I were second cameramen. They'd rent the studio for a week, and it took six days to make a picture. The week started Monday morning and ended at midnight Saturday. At ten to twelve every Saturday, Jaffe would walk in and say, "Wrap it up," even if the picture wasn't finished.

Then they rented the studio again for the next picture, for a week. They would put up little pieces of set in the corner of their stage and finish last week's picture.

They used to sell states rights to the picture. In other words, Schulberg had a sales force in New York, and he would get a contract for a picture. He would contract to pay a good actor a week's salary for two days' work, but by the time he was ready to make the picture, he hadn't spent a nickel. He sent the contracts on to New York, and New York went to a particular group who owned six or seven theaters in New Jersey, or another group in New Hampshire, and they would sign contracts and say, "On a certain date we will hand you a picture for your six theaters, and you pay us so much money." If a picture cost $200,000 they'd make $100,000 before they ever turned a camera. They sold the pictures before they were made, on the strength of the names. They were smart!

I hooked up with a cameraman named Ernie Haller and did a couple of films with him. One of them was *Stella Dallas*. That was 1925. Samuel Goldwyn was the producer, and he and Joe Schenck were good friends. As the story goes, at poker one night, Joe Schenck said to Sam Goldwyn, "I've got a very expensive cameraman on my hands. He's getting paid, but we're not shooting right now. Why don't you take him off my hands, since you're shooting a picture?" They were heartless. They fired Ernie Haller, and put Arthur Edeson on. Edeson said to me, "There's no reason why you should go," so I stayed on the picture.

Ernie went to New York and eventually got a contract. I went back to New York to join him. We did two pictures, *Reckless Lady*, and another one.

The important thing was that we had a director named Howard Higgin. After the second picture, on which I was second cameraman, Howard Higgin invited me to dinner at his home, and said, "With your personality, you're wasting your time on the camera. Why don't you become an assistant director?"

Again, being a typical New York kid, all I said was, "How much?" I was getting seventy-five dollars a week as a second cameraman, but by this time my camera was obsolete. I had to rent a Bell and Howell. I could make seventy-five a week clear as an assistant director. So I took the job. I did a picture starring Ben Lyon and Dorothy Mackaill, *The Dancer of Paris,* which Al Santell directed. He was the man who had lent me the money to go to New York in the first place.

ATKINS: Did most of these directors go back and forth from Hollywood to New York?

JACOBSON: They were sent for by the producers. The producer on this picture was Robert T. Kane.

An interesting thing happened. In 1926, B. P. Schulberg took over Paramount, and took Clara Bow and Sam Jaffe, who was the production manager, with him. Schulberg and Jaffe owned Paramount, so to speak, and I was still not in their good graces.

I was in New York, and a cousin of mine said, "Would you like to go to a dance?" I went, and before the evening was over he said to me, "There's a girl over there who wants to dance with you."

We danced. Her name was Mildred Gershowitz. She said, "Would you take me home when the dance is over?"

I said, "Sure," thinking romance.

On the way home she said, "Let's stop at Fleischer's," which was *the* place in Washington Heights. We stopped there, and she hit me right between the eyes with a question. She said, "Do you know Sam Jaffe?"

I said, "Yes, I do," and God was good; he tapped me on the shoulder, for I said the most glowing things about him. Then I said, "Why do you ask?"

She said, "He'll be here in the morning from California, and he wants to marry me. I met him a year ago, and he's been courting me. He wants to marry me tomorrow and take me back to California."

I said, "Do it."

She invited me to the party he was giving for her. I said I couldn't go. "I don't stand in good graces with him. If you want me to come to your party, he'll have to phone me."

Well, the next morning he phoned. "Why don't you stay out of my life?" was what he said, but I did go to the party.

Now, Mildred had a girlfriend, and during the party Sam suggested that the four of us go out on the town. We went to the Silver Slipper. Sam got drunker and drunker and I did a typical New York thing again. I hit him for a job while he was drunk. I knew that if I got in at Paramount, there would be a real steady job. He said, "Yes, sure, of course," in front of his bride-to-be.

I took my savings and went back on the train. Jaffe didn't see me for five days. He let me sit in the outer office. He sobered up, apparently, and realized what I had done, and didn't think it was very nice. Finally on the fifth day he saw me. He said, "I promised you a job, didn't I? What were you doing when I said that?"

I said, "I was an assistant director, making a hundred twenty-five dollars a week." I was getting the hundred twenty-five, but I hadn't really learned my business. I was faking it.

He said, "All right. I'm going to live up to my word. I'll give you a job. But while you're on the job, you have to prove yourself. You're not going to be a first assistant here until I know you're not the guy you were." He took me onto the backlot, and gave me a job on the swing gang, the dirtiest job in the studio, at twenty-seven dollars and fifty cents a week, plus overtime.

ATKINS: What is the swing gang?

JACOBSON: The set dressers take you to the bins and they say, "Take that chair and put it on the truck, and then drive the truck over to Stage 5 and put it there. Hang that picture on that wall." You never use your head.

On a Wallace Beery picture they had a junkyard. To get the junk, I went down Cahuenga Pass, shoveled garbage onto the truck, and took it to the Paramount Ranch.

I had to hold onto the job, and live on it for six months. I hated this man so, for doing this to me. I would never go near the front gate because I didn't want any of my friends to see me. I was very proud. They wouldn't allow you to go through the front gate to go across to Oblath's for lunch. You had to go way around through the Van Ness Avenue gate.

One day, while I was lifting a box, a voice said, "Artie, what the hell are you doing?" I turned around, and it was Bill Goetz, the William Goetz I had known in New York. We were very good friends. I told him the whole story.

Bill played poker with Schulberg that night. The next day, at lunch, I was approached at Oblath's, and when I went back to the studio I was a second assistant director to Bill.

We went to Lake Tahoe on a picture called *A Gentleman of Paris,* with Adolphe Menjou. The director was Harry D'Arrast. Bill and D'Arrast didn't get along, and Bill told me he was going to quit Paramount when the picture was finished. He also said, "I'll lay back, and you take over on the set. Make a big noise, and you'll get to be a first."

When we got back, D'Arrast was to do another picture immediately, and he went to Jaffe and asked for me as his assistant in place of Bill Goetz. So I became a first assistant.

Harry D'Arrast, who was a Frenchman, could not stand any arguments. It made him very nervous. He wasn't used to the producers and if things got a little rough, he'd just go home. He was an entirely different person.

ATKINS: Harry D'Arrast is one of those legendary names about whom not very much is known.

JACOBSON: He was a wonderful, wonderful man. He had worked in the cinema in France, and he became a very dear friend of mine. He came over here and got in with the Chaplin group. He became one of Charlie Chaplin's assistant directors. Chaplin had his own studio on La Brea Avenue in Hollywood, and as a result of it, Harry became a mystery man. Anyone who became connected with Charlie Chaplin became a mystery man.

Harry made some successful pictures, and he married the actress Eleanor Boardman. He was car-crazy, like most Frenchman. He bought a new French car, a Bugatti, and I bought his old car, a Will St. Claire, for one dollar. A short time later Harry disappeared, and the next thing I knew, he was back in France. When we went to make *Little Boy Lost* in Paris, I asked a lot of people about him. They said he had gone a little bit batty. He was peddling a script he had written, but no one would buy it. He finally passed away.

ATKINS: Did Harry D'Arrast have trouble getting a job in Hollywood after a certain time?

JACOBSON: No. I don't know why he left here. He did not get along with producers too well, because he couldn't stand their tactics. As I told you, instead of getting mad he'd get nervous and go home. Well, you don't go home in the middle of the day without getting a bad reputation.

ATKINS: What about Adolphe Menjou?

JACOBSON: I enjoyed working with him thoroughly. He was a great craftsman and was dependable. There were so many that I worked with, Mary Brian, Buddy Rogers, Richard Arlen, and a tall, skinny Englishman named William Austin.

There was also Jack Oakie. Here's how he came about: I knew a very nice guy from New York, a busboy at the Long Island studio, who became an assistant director and eventually a big producer. His name was Joe Pasternak. Joe was an assistant director at Universal with Wesley Ruggles. I used to live at the Regent Hotel on Hollywood Boulevard, and at night we'd all gather around and talk. This kid was there who was very funny. We went in the hotel and had a cup of coffee and he said, "I need work." I said I'd see what I could do, and the next day I called Joe Pasternak. I'd heard they were using lots of extras, soldiers, in a scene. I asked if he'd give him a job. "Sure. What's his name?"

"Jack Oakie," I told him. So Jack went to see Joe, and got a job, as a private, in a picture starring Laura La Plante. Wesley Ruggles was the director.

When Jack got home that night, he had a call-back. He said, "I don't know where they get those guys to do small parts. There's a scene where Laura La Plante is hiding. She's in a soldier uniform, standing in the ranks. A guy in back of her spits a BB through his teeth and hits her in the back of the neck. But he couldn't do it!".

I said, "You can do it. Tomorrow, don't ask anybody. Just do it."

Next day he came back and said, "Mr. Pasternak said I was very, very good." The following day he met Wesley Ruggles, and before the picture was finished Ruggles had put him under personal contract.

ATKINS: You worked on *Feel My Pulse,* in 1928, which Gregory La Cava directed.

JACOBSON: That was with Bebe Daniels. There's nothing to say about it.

ATKINS: Is there — or was there — a great difference between the duties of a first and second assistant director?

JACOBSON: Oh, there's a lot of difference. In those days, the first assistant ran the show, and the second assistant was more or less a gofer. Not today. Today they have a lot to do. There was a unit manager, who would watch over the money, find locations, and whatnot. The first assistant director took the script, broke it down, cross-plotted it, and with the various departments, made the budget. Then, when you went on the stage, you directed everything but the actors. You picked the extras and directed them and got along with the director. You were his right arm.

ATKINS: You had already worked with some well-known directors, including Henry King. Did you notice a great difference in them?

JACOBSON: Every director was an individual personality. To illustrate: Frank Borzage, who did *A Farewell to Arms,* was an Italian, although you'd never know it. He was a quiet-spoken, easygoing person. You wouldn't even know he was the director if you walked on the set. He never raised his voice. He just smoked his pipe, but he did his job.

Henry King was king of all he surveyed, but very nice. He was *the* director. He ran that set the way he wanted to.

In the early silent days, directors knew their business. They knew where to put the camera, and what to tell the actors to do. Of course in the early days, the minute an actor opened his mouth, they cut to a title. Then when they came back, his mouth closed. They said some very strange things while you were shooting the picture, but the cutter took care of it.

In 1926, I was a first assistant director at Paramount. We had no guild, so I did pictures like *A Farewell to Arms* in 1932 for sixty-five dollars a week, with no overtime, or benefits. We used to work an average of twenty-six hours a day, nine days a week! We never stopped.

ATKINS: Were you punching a time-clock in those days?

JACOBSON: No. When I became an assistant director, there were no time-clocks. We did a film called *Manpower* with Richard Dix. We made it on the old Paramount Ranch, which is now Forest Lawn, right behind Warner Bros.

The gist of the story was that a dam broke. Richard Dix was the guy who drove the tractor into the breach to stop the water from rushing down and engulfing the whole valley. We had wonderful special effects men, and we had four cameras on a platform at night down in the valley shooting up at the set. For some strange reason they let one "dump tank" go with the water to come rushing through. They always waited until it was just about finished before they let the second one go. They got half the first tank going, and they let the second one go. Well, all hell broke loose! That water hit down below; it hit the camera platform, and everybody on the platform. The lights went helter-skelter.

The stuntman for Richard Dix was swept down. Everybody said, "Where the hell is Chick Collins?" I don't know how many men grabbed the platform and lifted it, but he was under the platform. His nose was full of sand, and he would have been asphyxiated if we hadn't caught him.

In the meantime, our assistant cameraman had been hurt. I drove him to Hollywood Presbyterian Hospital, on Vermont, where they wanted me to fill out certain papers before they'd accept him, even though it was an emergency. I had a hell of a fight with the people there. But in those days, many people never paid their bills. That was *Manpower*.

ATKINS: Was there a lot of location and ranch shooting?

JACOBSON: A lot of ranch shooting, but not so much location shooting as we know it today. It was too expensive. You couldn't. You rarely went abroad. In many cases you went with a four man crew, and shot longshots with doubles, that's all.

ATKINS: Clarence Badger is another director about whom there doesn't seem to be very much information.

JACOBSON: We all loved him. He was the quietest man I've ever known, but he was a typical motion picture director. He was gray-haired, wore a cap and plus-fours with golf stockings. He always wore dark glasses, so nobody ever knew what color his eyes were. He never said anything. As his assistant, I would have to go and crouch down alongside of him, and he'd tell me what to do. But he never raised his voice. That was Clarence Badger! He was very highly respected, and he made good pictures. He made some very funny comedies, with Bebe Daniels and people like that.

ATKINS: Didn't he do one of the Clara Bow pictures?

JACOBSON: Yes, but not with me. I don't really know what happened to him.

ATKINS: You worked on *Children of Divorce,* with Clara Bow.

JACOBSON: That picture was with Gary Cooper, Clara Bow, and Esther Ralston. Frank Lloyd, a highly respected and successful director, was in charge. For some reason, the picture did not jell. It didn't turn out properly.

They hired a man named Josef von Sternberg to go in and look at it. I think he wrote seven days of added scenes, for stuff that they were going to throw out and replace. This was a tough job because Gary Cooper, Clara Bow, and Esther Ralston were all working in their own pictures.

Sam Jaffe said to me, "It's your job to figure it all out so that they don't work day and night. You've got to get with the assistant directors on the other three pictures and lay out a schedule so that you can get your work done without interfering with those pictures — and not tire out the actors."

It was a job! It meant that Joe von Sternberg, James Wong Howe, and I worked twenty-four hours a day for seven days. We never went home; we never quit shooting. Whenever we could get the actors between scenes, we'd rush them over, change their clothes, and do their scenes. Jimmy Howe used to fall asleep at the camera. He'd put his eye in it, look at something, and go to sleep. I'd go over and wake him up.

As a result of it, von Sternberg became a director for Paramount. The big thing he got was a picture called *Underworld.* From then on, you couldn't even talk to him. He became the biggest director ever.

Von Sternberg did one thing in *Children of Divorce* which caused quite a rumble. They thought he was a great genius. In the picture, Bow dies. She's lying in the bed, and the light from the window is on her. All of a sudden you see the shade being pulled down. The light went down, and she died. Well! They thought this was the greatest thing. Since then it's been done five million times.

ATKINS: Would he have thought of that on the set?

JACOBSON: Either that or he stole it from somebody. Who knows? He was at the right place at the right time.

ATKINS: Were the other films being made on the same lot?

JACOBSON: Oh, yes.

ATKINS: Did you go to see most of the pictures you worked on?

JACOBSON: Sure. I was very proud of them. During those years we all fought for screen credit. We would give up money if we could get screen credit. We could never get it, until we had the Screen Directors Guild.

ATKINS: Do you remember the year?

JACOBSON: No, I don't. We started in 1937. I know I got screen credit in 1940, though that wasn't through Paramount. I got it because I knew the producer — it was a personal thing. If you worked for an independent company, you could ask for screen credit when you took the job. Sometimes they'd bargain with you and cut ten bucks off your salary. It was tough making a living.

ATKINS: Can you tell me a little more about von Sternberg?

JACOBSON: He discovered Marlene Dietrich, and made a great star out of her, but he reached a point where he was untouchable.

By the way, no one was ever allowed to talk to Marlene. All that time she and von Sternberg were together she was still married to her husband who was a sick man. She brought him over from Germany and bought him a chicken ranch in the Valley.

Unfortunately, von Sternberg was about as disliked a man as you could find. He put on a great, great front. He dressed the part. He proceeded to grow a Fu Manchu moustache. He directed with a baton, like a musical director. Everybody was dirt under his feet. He was *it.* When we made *American Tragedy* and went to Lake Arrowhead to shoot the sequence where the boy drowns the girl, eighty percent of the people were frightened of him. When he said, "Quiet," you could hear a pin drop. If it did drop, it was just too bad for whoever dropped the pin.

Les White, the second cameraman, didn't like him because von Sternberg had belittled and insulted him. Les was a big man who could have broken von Sternberg in half.

Lee Garmes, the first cameraman, said to Les, "Easy does it. This will come to an end, too."

They were doing the scenes in the boat, and only four people could go: the two actors, Phillips Holmes and Frances Dee, in the bow of the boat; von Sternberg and Les White in the stern.

Von Sternberg showed up that morning dressed in a Russian fur hat, a mackinaw jacket, corduroy pants, high mountain-hiking boots, and a cane — on a hot summer's day. As he started to step into the boat, Les White said, "Mr. von Sternberg, I suggest you take those boots off."

"Why, pray tell me?"

"You never know what will happen in a boat. We're going out in the middle of the lake. I presume you can swim."

Von Sternberg looked at him suspiciously, but he took the boots off. He looked ridiculous. His legs were like match-sticks. They went out, and strangely, the minute they got in the middle of the lake, the motor of the boat caught fire. They had to rush in.

The girl I eventually married was an extra in the picture. One day, I came into the lobby, and she was sitting there with a rose in her hand. I said, "Gloria, what's with the rose?"

She said, "The king, the high lama, went through, and there was a rose in a vase on a table over there. He stopped, picked up the rose, came back and gave it to me. I said, 'Thank you. What's that for?' He said, 'Yours is the only smile I've gotten since I've been up here.'"

Later on, after he had been out of work for a long time and was doing a picture called *The Shanghai Gesture,* I went on the set one day. This is what I saw: he was sitting on a chair, and behind him on an easel was a blackboard. If you wanted to talk to him, you had to write your name on the blackboard. Eventually he would look at it and say, "Oh, Jacobson? What is it?" When I went over to him, the prop man would put a line through my name, which meant I had been given an audience with the Pope.

ATKINS: You talked about how you laid out everything for certain directors. Could you do this with von Sternberg?

JACOBSON: Yes. You had to lay out the whole thing. Otherwise they could never estimate how long the picture would take, or how much it was going to cost, or which actors were needed for what length of time. Once this was accomplished, you started shooting the picture.

But many times you'd go on the set, and things would change. Let's say you schedule a hundred fifty extras. The day before you shoot, the director says, "I want it more crowded."

"We don't have the money."

"I won't shoot it, then."

Sometimes I'd get with a director like Wesley Ruggles, who'd say, "How many people are we going to use?"

I'd say, "How do you see this nightclub? Is it successful? Is it crowded? Is there no place on the dance floor for another couple? Or are they losing their shirts, and the place is empty? I'll give you the picture you have in mind. Don't worry about how many people."

That night I would get the set dressers in. I could move four tables out, and squeeze some tables in, and it looked the same. Taking four tables out meant you took out sixteen people. Not using sixteen people for seven days could save a lot of money. But I always saw to it that my boss knew about it.

ATKINS: Was von Sternberg one of the people who would let you do certain things?

JACOBSON: No. No, no, no. He had everything his way. He was just plain mean.

In later days, after he had lost out, I would see him at the Guild's annual meeting every year. He was always off in a corner. He called me over the first time, and said, "Why doesn't anyone ever come over and say 'hello' to me? Incidentally, somebody wrote a book and said I was a dirty bastard when I was a director. Is that true?"

I said, "You were worse than that. You were the worst bastard that ever was. Nobody wanted to work with you. They had to work for you because the studio assigned them. You even upset people who never got upset, like Clive Brook."

Clive had told him off once. He was a quiet, staid Englishman who lost his temper and ripped von Sternberg to pieces.

ATKINS: Did he get out of the business because actors didn't get along with him?

JACOBSON: No. It was because some of the pictures didn't make money. He lost out at Paramount the first time because he made a picture with Marlene, and when they looked at the rushes, there was nothing but closeups of her. That led to a fight between the producer and von Sternberg, and first thing you know, there was no next picture.

If the pictures had been making money, no one would have cared. They said they cared, but they really didn't. For instance, people would come in and complain to Zanuck about Henry Hathaway. Zanuck would say, "You're absolutely right." Then when he saw Hathaway, he'd say, "Go on making good pictures, baby."

ATKINS: In 1927, you worked on a picture called *Afraid to Love,* which Edward H. Griffith directed.

JACOBSON: Arthur Lubin was an actor in that. Loretta Young played Florence Vidor's fourteen-year-old daughter.

ATKINS: Anything you recall about Edward Griffith?

JACOBSON: Yes, skipping to 1939 — I was promoted to looking for new talent. I was in New York, and Griffith came to the Paramount Building, told me about a kid he had met in Virginia, and said he would bring him up to meet me. The kid turned out to be a handsome blond giant named Sterling Hayden. I arranged for him to go to California, get a contract, and start acting. Griffith made him the lead in a picture he was making.

ATKINS: What about *Sawdust Paradise?*

JACOBSON: Luther Reed directed that. He was a writer first. Esther Ralston and Hobart Bosworth were in it. Reed Howes, who liked to imbibe, was the lead. We had a scene one night on the backlot where the whole carnival catches fire. Esther was up on one of those things, in a flimsy outfit, doing whatever she was supposed to do. Reed Howes was supposed to run in, grab her, and come running back through the flames, past camera. We had a path figured out, and the cameras were in set spots, so we didn't have to use a double. This was a scene which you couldn't do over again, because the set would be destroyed. When we went to midnight lunch, I went with him and kept my eye on him. Somebody called me, and I had to go back to the set to check on something. Everyone came back, and everything was all set. We were sure he hadn't been drinking. We stood him right by the camera. We checked everything, and gave the cue to the special effects men, to put the torch to the set. There must have been seven or eight of them and they all did it at the same time. It was very spectacular. I touched Howes' shoulder, which was his cue to run in and do his stuff, and in he went. He was supposed to run up and get her and turn, but he just stood there. We kept yelling at him, "Reed, get her and come down!" By this time the flames were getting close. One of the boys yelled, "Get Ralston!" and one of the grips ran in and got her. Howes just stood there. I ran in, got him and brought him back. He didn't know what was going on. He had been drinking, after all, and the heat of the flames had gotten to him. While he stood there, we just watched the whole goddamned set burn down. I don't think Mr. Howes ever worked again. A story like that takes about one-and-a-half minutes to go through the industry. It cost a lot of money. They had to rebuild the set. Esther Ralston was a delightful lady.

ATKINS: What happened to Luther Reed?

JACOBSON: I don't know. I hadn't thought about him all these years. But that happens all the time. Somebody will flare up and disappear.

ATKINS: You worked on another film with a director I'm not familiar with: *Someone to Love,* directed by F. Richard Jones.

JACOBSON: He was a very clever director from the school of the Keystone Kops, and he did a lot of funny pictures. I think he had a severe illness, because he always used to sit in a chair bent over with pain in the stomach. I think it was cancer, but I'm not sure. I liked him very much. We were doing a picture with Buddy Rogers and Mary Brian. As for Buddy Rogers, I think everybody knows everything there is to know about him. He could play every instrument that was ever built, and still can. Mary Brian was a dear girl, and still is. She's married to the head of the Paramount editorial department, Chuck West. She married him many years ago, and I see them every once in a while whenever there's some kind of a Paramount get-together.

The early years of my career were those of learning, making contacts, and establishing myself in the film industry.

Talkies

ATKINS: What is your recollection of the beginnings of sound pictures?

JACOBSON: For the first couple of days we were frightened — we didn't know what to expect. At first, the mysterious soundmen were kings, but we were very proud that we were able to understand them, considering all the commotion that they made on the set. When sound became widely used and we had done away with a lot of the mystery, we said to the soundmen, "Look, do it our way."

ATKINS: Paramount was not one of the first studios to use sound.

JACOBSON: In a way it was. The first studio was Warner Bros., but Paramount had sound before MGM. MGM made a picture called *Alias Jimmy Valentine.* For the great scene where he rubs his fingers with sandpaper, and opens the vault to save the child's life, MGM built a set at Paramount, because they had sound, and photographed the sequence there. That was the first thing I remember that Paramount did.

There were quite a few pictures where only a few sequences had sound. We started working on a silent picture, *Chinatown Nights,* which starred Wallace Beery and

Florence Vidor. The director was William Wellman. We were doing most of it on the backlot at night.

After about three or four days of shooting, we got to a scene where Wally and Florence walked the length of a whole block. The next day when we came to the set, we were notified to go home. Sound had come in, and the picture was cancelled until further notice. Because we all worked at that studio, we didn't scatter but we were curious. I tried to find out what was going on, but I couldn't. There were all kinds of rumors — a motion picture studio was the king of the rumor factories. Then we were notified to go back to work, and that it was going to be with sound. We re-rehearsed the long walking scene, and now it was going to be with words coming from the actors' mouths, not titles.

We had an awful lot of people and a lot of equipment we'd never seen before. There was a man sitting at a little desk with things on his ears. We found out that was a mixing panel. They'd strung all these piano wires over the actors' heads, the whole length of the block. We were doing it off a Western dolly, which is nothing more or less than a board on wheels with the cameras on it. The director usually sat on it. When the rehearsal was over, Wellman turned to the sound people and said, "How was that? All right? Let's go."

The man said, "No, no, not yet, Mr. Wellman. I'll have to ask you to do one thing: you see, we've got microphones set up at certain distances. Let them walk without talking, and when they get under a microphone let them stop, say what they have to say, and then continue on."

Wellman said, "You mean walk, stop, talk, walk, stop? What kind of scene do you think that'll look like? That's ridiculous. I can't make a scene like that. Why can't they talk all the time?"

"Because they'll get out of the range of the microphone."

Wellman said, "Well, can't you pull the microphone with them? And incidentally, why do the microphones have to be over their heads? Why can't I just hold it in my lap?"

He tried pulling the microphone. Then we had to stop while they put vaseline on the wires. Finally he said, "Take that particular microphone down, and hook it up and give it to me."

Then he sat down cross-legged under the camera on the dolly. He put the microphone right in his crotch, and said, "Get me a pillow ", and they got him a pillow.

The guy said, "No, the microphone has to be over there."

Wellman said, "Why?"

The fellow said, "Well, according to the 'dbs' —."

Wellman said, "Come on, let's go. Can you understand what they're saying?"

The soundman said, "I can understand it, but the quality —."

Wellman said, "Artie, roll it."

We rolled it, and the guy started again with the "dbs." Wellman said, "Print it We'll talk about it again tomorrow night."

The next day we went in to see the rushes. There was nothing wrong with the scene. We heard everything they had to say, and there were no background noises that we didn't want. The soundman hadn't come to the projection room. When Wellman came on the set he said, "You did a good job. That's the way we're going to do the rest."

The soundman said, "No, we can't, Mr. Wellman."

"We'll get somebody else. If you can't do it, I'll get somebody who can, because you just did it."

That's the way sound started.

ATKINS: You've related something that's quite different from the stories one usually hears about cameras in booths, or "ice boxes."

JACOBSON: Did you ever hear of blankets. Every blanket in town was around the cameras. All you saw was a little piece of glass. Even the cameramen's heads were under the blankets. That was before we had blimps. Now, as far as the ice boxes were concerned, it was hell in there. It was hot, it was mean, and nobody outside could hear us and we couldn't hear them.

A very strange thing happened. When sound came in they built four new stages at Paramount — 11, 12, 13, and 14, way back, opposite the music department. We were going to shoot a picture with Dorothy Arzner there the next morning. We went back to look at it, and, as we approached the stage, we saw smoke billowing out of the big doors. Before morning, the four stages had burned right to the ground. They had to rebuild them, and while they were doing that, all the other stuff in the studio had to switch over and work at night because the noise of building the new stages would penetrate the stages.

During the fire, a grip and I tried to help. We had things with fire hoses, and we took them down and screwed them onto a hydrant. It was no good, because it was a phony hydrant.

When morning came, after we'd all helped, my clothes, which I could ill afford, had little burn holes in them. So I went to my boss, Sam Jaffe, and said, "Look, Sam, I'm going to have to have these clothes replaced."

He said, "By whom?"

I said, "By the studio."

He said, "What's your job?"

"Assistant director."

"You're not a fireman, are you?"

"That's right."

He said, "Why don't you mind your own business."

ATKINS: You did do a picture with Dorothy Arzner?

JACOBSON: Two. One was back on Long Island in 1930, called *Honor Among Lovers.* The other was with Clara Bow and Freddie March, *The Wild Party.*

Let me tell you something about Long Island. For some strange reason, somebody got the idea that we were doing pictures in a much more efficient way in Hollywood than they were there, so they sent two of us back to show them how to do it. It was the worst thing they could do to us — the people in New York hated us, because we were from the Coast.

They sent me to do a picture with George Cukor, called *The Royal Family of Broadway,* with a great Broadway star, Ina Claire, who played the part based on Ethel Barrymore. Fredric March played the part based on John Barrymore. This was 1930.

I sent for my fiancee, so we could get married. She arrived on a Sunday, and I didn't realize that you can't get married in New York on a Sunday. I told her to stay home, and Monday morning we went to work at the studio.

There was going to be a week of rehearsals, because Cukor had been a stage director. We sat around, as they say, reading the jokes. There were Mary Brian and Charlie Starrett, etc. About ten o'clock in the morning we got to the point where the dialogue revealed the fact that Mary Brian, who was playing Ina Claire's daughter, was pregnant.

Ina Claire held her hand up and said, "Hold everything, George." They were good friends. "Wait a minute. What's this pregnancy? When I signed a contract to do this part nobody ever told me that I was going to be a grandmother. I don't want to play a grandmother, or even a potential grandmother."

Cukor, being the kind of guy he was, just turned to me and said, "Artie, nine o'clock tomorrow morning, right here. Ina, come on up to the office. Everybody dismissed."

I got married that afternoon. Now who knows? If that hadn't happened, maybe I never would have gotten married.

When that picture was finished, instead of sending me back to the Coast, they kept me there to do *Honor Among Lovers*, which I didn't want to do. I hated it back there.

There was an interesting thing about *The Royal Family of Broadway*. Cukor got the idea. The famous scene in that picture is when the Barrymore character comes home from wherever he's been around the world. He comes in like a wild man with all kinds of crazy things. He goes up a winding staircase, undressing as he goes up. By the time he gets to the top, just as he slips his shorts off, leaving him stark naked, he's into the bathroom. We didn't have such things as camera cranes in 1930, so we had to figure out how to do it.

George Folsey, George Cukor, and I all got together and tried to figure what to do. Somebody came up with the idea of going to a milling company, where they take grain and make flour out of it. They had the strangest looking forklift, with a big wide bed on it, where they'd pile numerous sacks of grain. It was a big heavy thing, but it would go up. So, by God, we decided to try to use it as a camera platform.

They brought it to the studio in Long Island. Going up and down was fine because it was electric, but it couldn't go forward or back or sideways, except by manpower. We had about twenty men pushing it and we got the shot. That may have been the forerunner of the camera crane. Who knows?

ATKINS: How did it look on the screen?

JACOBSON: Fine. Nobody knew what we had used.

ATKINS: Fredric March had come from the stage, hadn't he?

JACOBSON: Yes. He was in the play, *The Royal Family*. He was on the road, traveling with the show. He came to San Francisco, when we started to cast *The Wild Party*. The dialogue director was Robert Milton, a cute little man. They wanted Fredric March to play the professor at a college where Clara Bow was a wild coed. They bought the show out for as long as the picture was going to last, brought him down and put him in the movie. That was the beginning of Fredric March in movies. He was a prototype of John Barrymore. He walked like him, talked like him, damn near looked like him.

ATKINS: He did seem to resemble Barrymore in later years.

JACOBSON: He dropped the strange walk and everything because the parts didn't call for that. But it made him outstanding, unusual. He was a very good actor and a very nice guy, married to a wonderful woman.

ATKINS: Can you tell me a little more about *Honor Among Lovers* and about Dorothy Arzner?

JACOBSON: I'll tell you who played a bit in it, and it was her first picture — Ginger Rogers. One of the most beautiful women I've ever laid my eyes on also played a bit — Avonne Taylor. I learned later that she was a very dear friend of one of the high, high muckamucks at Paramount, in the banking business.

All I can tell you about Dorothy Arzner is that I thought she was great. She was a very quiet woman. She always wore dark glasses and mannish clothes. She had been a film cutter, and she became a director. She never threw her weight around, but she knew her business, and I enjoyed working with her thoroughly.

ATKINS: There's been so much discussion about women directors and their problems. Did she have any difficulty asserting her authority?

JACOBSON: Let me put it to you this way. She came by train, and it was rumored around the studio in New York that a woman was going to direct. Well, this was unheard of, and those guys in New York were pretty tough and rough. I tried to smooth it as much as I could. One of them said to me, "A broad gonna direct?" and I told him, "She's just as good as any man." He said, "That I gotta see."

I'd already done a picture with her, so the morning that she arrived, which was on a Sunday, I picked her up at the station and took her to the hotel. We sat down to eat lunch, and I said, "I just have one thing to say, Dorothy," and she said, "I know what you're going to talk about. I'm a woman. This is New York. They don't understand."

I said, "That's right. They will understand the minute they see you work. But, whatever you do, Dorothy," — and I told George Seaton this too, when he did his first feature — "do me a favor. Just direct. If anybody comes to you with a question that has nothing to do with actual direction, send him to me. That's my job. Because once you answer one question, they're all going to be on you. Just be the mystery woman."

She said, "That sounds great to me."

After the first day she had won their confidence. She knew exactly what she wanted, the minute she walked in. She lined up the cameras, and did whatever she needed. Then we went to lunch, came back and shot it. She didn't screw around. Consequently it was a very nice thing.

ATKINS: Was it easy for her in Hollywood?

JACOBSON: Oh, yes. There was no resistance there. Because the people — the cameramen, the assistant director — completely surrounded her. You couldn't break through our wall and be nasty, because we knew that she knew her business, and we were able to answer all the questions, which made the work easy for the boys. They didn't have to move a wall in and have someone say, "Well, wait a minute. Move it out again. Wait a minute. Move it back."

The worst thing you could do, or still do, is have the director walk in, not having done his homework, not knowing what he wants to do. The company senses it, and they lean back, waiting for him to make up his mind. No, she had no problem. Everybody liked her. Everybody respected her. That was the important thing.

ATKINS: Had she been a cutter at Paramount or another studio?

JACOBSON: She was a cutter at Paramount for many years. We didn't know her as a cutter. Very few cutters came on the set in those days, except when the new directors started to come in, and they wanted them on the set. For instance, when we went back to New York to do *Royal Family of Broadway,* we had co-directors, George Cukor and Cyril Gardner. Cyril Gardner was a cutter, but George had such a strong personality, that he directed the actors and the actresses, and Cyril saw to it that the camera was put in the right place so he'd be able to cut the film. By the time the thing got started, nobody even knew that Cyril was around.

Funny thing about Cyril: he was very superstitious. He went to Europe, and went to some seer who told him never to cross the water, so he never came back. He wouldn't get on a boat. That was the last we ever heard of him.

ATKINS: You mentioned before that you were responsible for setting up the schedule; was this so with sound?

JACOBSON: The words on paper could not explain how long it was going to take to shoot, so we went right along, just as if sound had not come in, until we got a little experience.

Everything that happened before the picture started shooting came from the assistant director's plan. You made a plan in this manner: you read the script very, very thoroughly. You then did what we call a breakdown, which included every set that you needed, the actors who worked in that set, and whether that set was in the daytime or nighttime, because this affected the photography and the wardrobe. The music was also involved, because it had to be pre-recorded weeks before you ever photographed.

Then, when you got the thing completely broken down, you made what is known as a cross-plot board — a plan of how you're going to shoot. Scene 1, 40, and 90 may all be in the same spot, so you put all those scenes together. Once all those scenes were shot, you had to tear that set down, or take it down and put it aside, to make room for other sets.

The plan controlled the building of the sets, and showed the wardrobe department when costumes were needed. They had to be ready before the stage was, so that they could be tested. The transportation department had to know the schedule, especially if there was location shooting: how many cars and trucks were needed, for instance. The commissary had to know the day before you were shooting how many lunches to provide.

Let us say you had a picture that took thirty-six days. By the time you got through with the board, you knew when all the actors worked. The star might work all thirty-six days, while actors in small parts might work the first three days and not again until the last three days. We had to tell the actors specifically what we were going to do the next day, so that they could study the lines, which they were not used to doing unless they happened to be stage people that we had drafted into the movies. If they came in the morning and didn't know their words and said, "Nobody told me what to study," it was my responsibility. If a thing like that happened to an assistant director twice, that was it. He'd be working somewhere else, or not at all.

You had to tell the casting office, which made the arrangements for contracts with the actors' agents. Some actors, if they were important enough, got paid from the moment they started until they finished, even though there was a week or two when they didn't work. Otherwise their salaries were pro-rated. You made arrangements so that they were available when they were needed. You might okay letting an actor who was only appearing in the first and last scenes take another job in between. If the schedule had to be changed because someone got sick it got to be quite a mishmash. So you needed that cross-plot, and you had to stick to it.

ATKINS: What about the contract players?

JACOBSON: They were paid hot or cold, but their salaries were charged to that one picture.

Something else from the standpoint of physical production — when you went on location you could not cut out the background sounds.

They developed a thing called dubbing. You made the scenes and the actors spoke their lines, but after the picture was finished shooting, you went back in and recorded those same lines without the background sounds. Many directors didn't like that, because it took a long, long time for them to be able to record an actor's lines, and it had a dead sound. It didn't sound like outdoors. We used to make all kinds of sound effects tracks, like automobile horns, dub them in, and sort of blend them into the other scenes.

If you ran into a star actor who couldn't memorize his lines, it could take you twice as long to do a day's work as it did without the sound.

ATKINS: Were there any big actors who had trouble memorizing lines?

JACOBSON: At the very beginning it cost a few of them their careers. I told you about Clara Bow and how it ruined her career. But by the same token, for actors who came from the stage, it proved a great advantage, because once it became known that an actor was a good study, people would say, "Let's use him."

One thing happened at Paramount. The directors knew where to put a camera, but a lot of them didn't know what to do with actors when they had to speak. B. P. Schulberg got an idea. He imported quite a few directors from various places around the country, and we had two directors on every picture: one to place the camera and take care of the action, and the other to be sure that the actors performed properly, vocally. George Cukor came from that, as did quite a few others.

ATKINS: One of the people was Rowland V. Lee.

JACOBSON: He was a small, very mild-looking writer, who became a director. He looked like a bookkeeper, but he had GUTS! Everybody respected him. He made a lot of Pola Negri pictures. He could get along with her. He made a lot of Fu Manchus also.

ATKINS: *The Mysterious Dr. Fu Manchu* is listed as a "Movietone," so it must have been a sound film.

JACOBSON: Oh, yes, there was sound in it. As a matter of fact, there was what you called a bad study: Fu Manchu himself, Warner Oland. Rowland V. Lee had no sympathy for him. Warner would come in and he just couldn't remember the words. Of course the minute one actor didn't know his words, or forgot them, or stumbled, after four or five tries the other actors started to do the same.

ATKINS: You worked on other Fu Manchu films at about the same time.

JACOBSON: I did three or four of them, but I can't remember one from the other because they were all the same: same cast, same director. Warner Oland was always Fu. The boy was Neil Hamilton, the girl was Jean Arthur, and O. P. Heggie was the detective.

ATKINS: You haven't said much about the actors and actresses you worked with: Gary Cooper, Mary Astor, and Douglas Fairbanks, Jr.

JACOBSON: Let's start with Mary Astor. We worked together at the Biograph studio. She was a beautiful 16-year-old child named Lucille Langehanke.

Her father, Otto Langehanke, was a wonderful guy. Her mother used to sew buttons on for us. Sometimes she'd cook at home and bring us decent food.

Our leading man was Glenn Hunter, a big star on Broadway.

ATKINS: What about Douglas Fairbanks, Jr., and *Stella Dallas*?

JACOBSON: I was the assistant cameraman on part of that. Belle Bennett was Stella Dallas, and Jean Hersholt played the drunk. The father was Ronald Colman. The two kids were Douglas Fairbanks, Jr., who was sixteen years old, and Lois Moran who played the girl he fell in love with. There was nothing special about that. Many years later, when I joined up with Rheingold in television and went to Europe, young Fairbanks was the producer. Small world.

ATKINS: Can you tell me something about Gary Cooper?

JACOBSON: I worked with him on a picture called *Devil and the Deep*. Tallulah Bankhead, Charles Laughton, and Cary Grant were also in it. Tallulah was something else, God bless her. Everybody loved her and she loved everybody.

We were working on the backlot, in a mock submarine. It was too hot to work during the day under those tarpaulins, so we switched everything and worked from six at night until eight in the morning. There was no air conditioning. Tallulah said to me, "That's the most wonderful guy I've ever known," meaning Cooper. Well, Coop couldn't care less about anything. He was so quiet and nice. Any gal he wanted to be with, nobody ever knew about, until press agents got after him. But she said, "By God, he won't pay any attention to me." One evening we broke for midnight lunch.

When I walked into the commissary I looked around, but Tallulah wasn't there. I walked back to the set with Coop. He went into his dressing room, and all hell broke loose. Instead of going to eat, she had gone into his dressing room and sat there waiting for him in the dark. When he walked in she jumped all over him. When he came streaking out, he was all smeared with lipstick. She was running after him with her dress hiked up over her knees, screaming, "Stop, you big — ." Cooper ran down the lot, followed by Tallulah, followed by me, because I didn't want them to break up the night's work. In those days, Cooper had a Duesenberg which he housed in a garage across the street from the studio. The garage later became Oblath's. By the time we got there, he had driven into the street. I jumped in my car and chased him into Beverly Hills. I jumped out of my car and into his at a red light, and said, "You can't do this. We can't lose a whole night's shooting." He said, "Will you keep her away from me?" I promised I would, and we both came back to the studio. She never tried it again, I must say.

Tallulah and Charles Laughton had known each other in England before he came to America. In this picture he played a half-demented submarine captain and she played his wife, who was fooling around with the characters played by Cooper and Grant. In one scene, she came home at four o'clock in the morning, and the captain confronted her and asked where she'd been. When she started to tell him, his line was, "Don't you talk that filth to me," and he slapped her. With Laughton's lips, every time he said the "f" of "filth," Tallulah was sprayed.

When Laughton had to do an emotional scene of any kind, he went into a corner, or into the spot where he was going to do the scene, turned his back to the whole company, and worked himself up into it. He and I got along fine. Right in the middle of his heaving shoulders, he'd give me a little signal, like Brando did in the later days, and we'd turn the camera over. Then he'd turn around and play the scene.

We were rehearsing this when out of her dressing room came a voice on a record singing, "I'll be down to get ya in a taxi, honey." The shoulders stopped. He called me over, and said, "Go tell that bitch — it can only be her — that I am rehearsing a scene, and to turn that thing off. Use those words — verbatim."

I went to her dressing room and said, "Tallulah, Mr. Laughton — ."

She said, "What does that —— want?"

I said, "He's trying to do a scene, and you're playing a record."

She said, "I want to play my record. If he's the actor he claims he is —," and she went on and on.

He started to rehearse again, and the record started again. I went to her dressing room again, and she said, "Oh, I got to him, eh?" She didn't play the record after that.

We got to the master scene where he has to slap her. Well, he slapped her, and he slapped her so hard he knocked her right out of the scene. We did four takes and each time he slapped her out of the scene. She never said "boo," but we had to go fix her face because you could see the finger marks.

Well, that took care of *Devil and the Deep*. There were no incidents between her and Cary Grant.

Here's an illustration of what I meant when I said we worked twenty-six hours a day. We had scenes where we had to go to the Paramount Ranch. It was supposed to be in Africa. This is where the first assistant director came in, because he planned it all. You would shoot all the night scenes as you went along. When you came to a big closeup, you skipped it. When night was over and daylight appeared, and the sun started to come up, you went back. You put a tarpaulin over that spot, and made the closeups, to match into the night stuff — so you could work that much longer.

ATKINS: You worked on several musicals. What was your job on those?

JACOBSON: My job was the same as on the other pictures, except that we had to deal with an added element.

ATKINS: I'm trying to pinpoint what might have been the first musical you worked on. It would have been *Paramount on Parade.*

JACOBSON: I only did pieces of *Paramount on Parade.*

ATKINS: What do you remember about it?

JACOBSON: It was directed by Leo McCarey. Somebody came up with the idea to use all the stars at Paramount, as well as all the directors and writers there. It wound up as eight blackouts, and ran about an hour and fifty minutes, a little longer than the ordinary picture of those days. Everybody was in it! Some of the stars were Iris Adrian, Jean Arthur, Mischa Auer, George Bancroft, Clara Bow, Evelyn Brent, Mary Brian, Clive Brook, Virginia Bruce, Nancy Carroll, Ruth Chatterton, and Maurice Chevalier. You had to coordinate your work with the other guys, so that when you needed the actors they weren't working in somebody else's sequence. *Paramount on Parade* was a big success.

ATKINS: Did the shooting of the film take up a lot of extra stage space?

JACOBSON: No, there were other pictures shooting. But that's planning. I told you about the breakdowns. For instance, every day at eleven o'clock in the morning every unit manager of each picture and all the studio department heads met in one room. They discussed what they had to do the next day, so they couldn't clash.

One of the most important people at those meetings was the woman who ran the commissary, because many times one picture would have a hundred fifty extras and another one would have three hundred extras. If both pictures broke for lunch at the same time there'd be no room. Everything was coordinated, but when anything went wrong there was chaos.

ATKINS: I understand that *Paramount on Parade* had color sequences. Had you worked on any other picture before that which had color?

JACOBSON: Yes. The only problem we had in color was that Technicolor assigned a man to the picture and he was on the set all the time. Every once in a while he became a pain in the rear, because he did his job. In other words he would walk up to you just before you shot a scene and would say, "You see that girl in the background there, with the yellow hat? The yellow hat's no good. It's too yellow. It will detract from everything else. They'll be playing a scene in the foreground, but your eye will be on the yellow hat."

Suppose the director says, "I like the yellow hat. I want it." But this man was responsible to Technicolor.

ATKINS: When I interviewed David Butler, he said it was Mrs. Kalmus who used to come on the set.

JACOBSON: Never. If you will look at every Technicolor picture, you will see that it says, "Color Coordinator," and his name. All the cameras belonged to Technicolor. You rented them. Except for the head cameraman, who did the lighting, Technicolor supplied the manpower — the camera operators and mechanics were all Technicolor men.

ATKINS: This was 1930. This was not the Technicolor that they developed later on, was it?

JACOBSON: No, this was two-strip, later it was what they called the 3-strip, which used tremendous cameras. Three pieces of film went through the camera at the same time. They were yellow, red, and blue. I don't know what they did back in the laboratory, because I never got interested in that part. Eventually it was simplified and it became one-strip. Then Eastman Kodak got into it, and developed a single-strip color, Eastman Color.

ATKINS: What about the lighting?

JACOBSON: The lighting was entirely different once the color came in. That was up to the cameraman. A lot of the cameramen who had never photographed films in color had to learn.

ATKINS: What about the idea of having part of the picture in color?

JACOBSON: It was very expensive, terribly expensive. But sometimes the producer, the director, and the writers would decide that it would be to the advantage of the picture to suddenly have one sequence in color.

There were some times when color hurt. For instance, my dear friend George Seaton always said, "This type of picture has got to be done in black-and-white. It's the dregs of New York. It's the East Side. How the hell are you going to make a garbage can full of garbage, how are you going to feel sorry for them in color?"

ATKINS: Which episodes of *Paramount on Parade* did you work on?

JACOBSON: I don't remember. Those of us who were lucky enough never stopped working. At this time, each studio was making at the very least a picture a week, fifty-two pictures a year. The theaters were eating them up, just like television today.

Many times if there were some retakes to be done on a picture and you were already working on another one, you'd do the retakes at night. You'd finish shooting your picture at six o'clock, run down and get a sandwich, run back and work until midnight on a picture you had finished last week. You were always working. To try to figure out which ones you had worked on was impossible.

There was a wonderful actor, who one day walked in and said his lines, but it turned out he was in the wrong studio — he'd gone to the studio where he had worked the day before.

ATKINS: How did you shoot the musical numbers?

JACOBSON: When we were making a musical, we could only have one sound track. You couldn't very well go back each time you wanted to make a two-shot, a closeup, an over the shoulder shot. Let's say that one number took six angles. With one sound track, how are you ever going to cut it together? So they had four cameras, completely soundproof, and then they cut the visual film to suit the track.

ATKINS: Were they using playbacks at that time?

JACOBSON: Always. In the musicals, everything had to be done to playback, that is, lip-synched. They never did what they called "direct recording," because you had to use other voices for actors who couldn't sing, and if you had somebody who could sing, the quality was very bad doing it out on a big stage. This way you took them on a music stage and all the acoustics were right.

Later on, say with Betty Hutton, they could do a song twelve times, but they'd only pick the good parts and put them all together. Music cutters were magicians, and still are.

ATKINS: There's some disagreement about when the use of playbacks began.

JACOBSON: As far as I'm concerned, ever since I got into sound in 1929, with *Chinatown Nights*, practically everything we did was a playback.

ATKINS: Did you have any responsibilities concerning the playback machines?

JACOBSON: No. The person that was added to the set was a music coordinator, like Arthur Franklin, who was responsible for the actors rehearsing properly.

After the song had been pre-recorded, and you got on the set, another man from the music cutting department was assigned to the music coordinator. His only job was to listen to the playback and look at the actor's mouth and say whether it was a hundred per cent in sync. You could get a beautiful take, acting-wise, but you'd always look over at him. If he shook his head, you wanted to kill him. He was a very unpopular guy, just like the assistant cameraman on Technicolor who said you had to do it again.

We had the music department before and during the shooting. By the time the picture was almost finished, the music composer came in and wrote the score, which was turned over to the music department for orchestration. Phil Kagan, the contractor for the orchestra, hired the musicians.

Then you had music sound recorders, and some of them were great. At Paramount we had a guy named Phil Wisdom who did a hell of a job, but he never opened his mouth.

After the music was recorded, you went into the dubbing room. You had anywhere from two to six men at the consoles. All these men had notes about where they would bring in special sounds, such as an automobile horn, which were running on separate tracks on dummies, which were in another building. They put together the sound effects and the dialogue and the music, and there was your movie.

ATKINS: Did you go to any dubbing sessions as an assistant director?

JACOBSON: No. First of all, the minute you finished a picture you were usually put on another one.

Later, when I became an associate with Perlberg and Seaton I not only went to them, I was responsible for them, for post-production. As a matter of fact, I was responsible for everything, from the time I woke up in the morning until I went to bed at night. Many times I'd go on location, like in Paris, and they had to leave early. When we shot in Tokyo — they didn't even go.

ATKINS: We talked about *Shoot the Works* before.

JACOBSON: Yes. It was Dorothy Dell's first picture. She played the lead, and she got killed right after she finished it.

After that we did *Wagon Wheels.* Charles Barton and I were always trying to get a job directing, because we were helping all kinds of schlock directors. Even if they were good, some of them were such drunks that you'd have to cover up, to do everything under the sun to pull them through.

The time came when they decided they were going to promote two of the guys — Charlie and me. We tossed a coin for the first picture and Charlie won it. He got *Wagon Wheels.* Then I did *Home on the Range,* which did not get good reviews.

The Assistant Director

ATKINS: Were you the assistant director on *Wagon Wheels*?

JACOBSON: No, I was the co-director, so to speak, without credit. That picture did very well.

ATKINS: Where would the fine line be between being co-director and being the first assistant?

JACOBSON: Oh, they were completely different. I worked with Charlie on the script, and had nothing to do with production at all. There was an assistant director there to do that.

There's a very heavy line, not a fine line between assistant director and director. One job is logistical, the other is creative. Actually, "assistant director" is a misnomer. You really are the stage manager. The only direction you ever do is the direction of extras, unless the director has great confidence in you — then he lets you go out and shoot second unit for him. If he's sick for a day, he'll talk the studio into letting you go ahead and be director for that day.

Eventually, over a period of years, I did a lot of directing. I directed the air stuff in *The Bridges of Toko-Ri*. I directed the second unit in many pictures.

ATKINS: What about the functions of the assistant director and the unit production manager?

JACOBSON: There again is a definite line of demarcation. A unit manager takes care of advance preparation, like setting locations. It's his job to make the deal with the people who own the location so that you can work there, and to see that, if necessary, a camp is set up for the whole company to live in. A company might run about sixty to seventy people. He has to see that you get the right food, and that everybody is paid properly. If you're going to stay in a hotel, he sees that everybody has the proper rooms.

As an assistant director, many times I have tangled with unit managers, because they like the idea of yelling "Quiet!" They butt in on your work. For instance, we were shooting in the commissary at Macy's Department Store, for *Miracle on 34th Street*. It was between Thanksgiving and Christmas, and it was so busy we could only shoot there for an hour . We were going to use the real people and augment them with extras, as the Guild required. We had everything all set up beforehand, but the unit manager on this picture was not a good one — he was somebody's friend, and that's how he got the job.

George Seaton and I had decided exactly what we wanted done. Edmund Gwenn was in line with a tray. I said, "We don't even need to rehearse it. Let's shoot it and save that time."

We shot it, and George said, "Cut! Artie, that's not what I wanted."

I said, "I know it's not. I don't know why they didn't do what I asked them to do." So I went to the extras and said, "Why didn't you — ?"

They said, "Well, that man there told us to do it this way."

The unit manager had gone in behind me and changed everything. So I said to George, "You'd better get him off the set or we're going to lose the whole day, because I'm going to walk. He's got his job — to get permission to shoot in the commissary, and to clean it up after we're through shooting. But when it comes to shooting a scene, it's you, I, and the cameraman." We straightened that out.

ATKINS: Weren't jobs like unit manager and production manager things that came into existence relatively late in movie history?

JACOBSON: Yes, because at the beginning you did the whole job yourself. But when picture-making started to spread, instead of everything being done within the studio lot, they got the idea that the picture should breathe a little. You could go on location and get some beautiful things. You used to send the location manager out, and that became a job, and a department. Because there were so many pictures being made, the location department became so busy that they could not attend to a particular picture. They hired a man to do it, and that man eventually became the unit manager. Not only did he find the location, but he was the advance man and the cleanup man.

Now the production manager, per se, was Sam Jaffe. He was the production manager of the entire studio, but he couldn't take care of each company. There were too many shooting at one time. He would hire an individual for each company, and they became a unit production manager. So the production manager was the high muckamuck who could hire and fire the unit manager, the assistant director, the second assistant director, et cetera. There was one at every studio, and he was responsible to the head of the studio for the cost of the picture.

That was another thing. Once the assistant broke it down, he turned all his material over to the unit manager, who in turn got with the various business departments, like accounting and insurance. Out of it would come the cost of the picture.

ATKINS: Was there a wide range of what assistants were getting paid?

JACOBSON: No. It was standard at each studio. The money was not big. A beginning guy would get maybe thirty-five dollars a week, because he was worthless except as a gofer. If you happened to be Frank Borzage's brother, Lew Borzage, and you were in your brother's contract, you got more. But you could get the jobs if you knew somebody. For instance, every time Sam would get a relative out here, I was stuck with him. We had one who used to eat apples and bet on the horses over the telephone. We had another who had been a butcher. They just didn't belong in the business.

If you were an old-timer, you were lucky to get an extra fifteen bucks a week. When I did *A Farewell to Arms* I was one of the top guys at Paramount. I was paid sixty-five dollars a week. I think that when the Guild first started to function, when we first were recognized, we got a hundred thirty-seven dollars and fifty cents, but no overtime.

On locations they would pay all of the expenses. We used to have arguments. For instance, when I worked on *I Wanted Wings,* they sent me to Texas. I said, "If I'm going to fly to Texas and I'm going to do all that flying down there, my personal insurance doesn't cover it. I expect the studio to cover me." They wouldn't do it.

But when the director said, "I won't go unless I get covered," they covered him. Well, that opened the door for us, and that's how we got insurance.

Another thing happened when we got the Guild: we got flight pay if we did anything in the air. We got so much per flight, not over three flights a day. In *I Wanted Wings* I did three flights a day for three weeks. That was a hundred five dollars a day over and above my salary.

Everything that happened to us that's good, including screen credit, is because of the Guild. The producers never gave us anything. When I say "the producers," I'm talking about the big studios.

When the Guild came in, it put an awful crimp in the use of relatives, too.

ATKINS: Tell a little more about the Guild.

JACOBSON: The Screen Directors Guild started in 1936 at the old Hollywood Athletic Club. Certain directors and assistants had dinner together and made a proposal to the producers which took three years to go through.

ATKINS; But the Guild had been formed. You're speaking about a contract?

JACOBSON; Yes. The Guild was just a bunch of guys getting together and saying, "We've got to make up our minds to get one thing: if we don't get it, we'll be in a position to strike." Now very few of us could do that. But we put on a big front.

ATKINS: Outside of the almost limitless hours, what were some of the other grievances?

JACOBSON: Oh, my gosh, everything. You couldn't get them to give you a raise, no matter what you did, no matter how hard you worked.

ATKINS: When you went to the ranch, for instance, did you have to provide your own transportation?

JACOBSON: Well, I did, because I always wanted to be able to get the hell out, and otherwise I'd have to wait until a car was full of people. But now you can't do that. The Teamsters won't let you. You must go in a studio car. The last time it happened to me, we were going out to Malibu, and I lived at Sunset and the beach. They came to me in the middle of the day and said, "Is that your car?"

"Yes."

"Well, don't bring it tomorrow. We have transportation for you. You're putting a driver out of a job."

"But I live right at the beach."

"Fine. Just be out in front and a studio car will pick you up and bring you back."

I never fought those unions. Everything union-wise came as a result of abuses. For instance, my wife was a dancer, and she was under contract to Warner Bros. They were so cheap that when the kids weren't dancing they used them as extras. The kids all needed the work, and didn't want to lose the steady jobs. They were doing a fight picture, and there was a scene where the ring was all lighted, and all the people were in darkness. They put all these kids and other extras in seats, then between all the kids they put dummies, and asked the dancing kids to put their arms around the dummies' shoulders and move the dummies around. There was such a stink about it, all that was cut out. Using the dancers as extras was cut out, also.

ATKINS: You don't hear about these things.

JACOBSON: No, of course not.

ATKINS: Getting back to *Wagon Wheels* — William Mellor was the cameraman.

JACOBSON: Yes. He became John Ford's cameraman. He was an assistant cameraman, and then became what is known as a camera operator — he actually operated the camera. The cameramen, like Leon Shamroy, did the lighting, picked the set-up, and decided which lens to use. When it came to actually shooting, there was the camera operator, and it's the same today. They're wonderful workers. Look at the football games. That's television, but think of how they can follow the plays. William Mellor became a first cameraman on *Wagon Wheels.*

ATKINS: You said you didn't want to talk about *Home on the Range,* but I read a good review of it in the *Motion Picture Herald.*

JACOBSON: I was so ambitious and so Paramount-oriented that I thought Paramount could do no wrong. I couldn't imagine them sending me in to my first directorial effort with a bad script. It wasn't even a bad script — the script wasn't written and they used to rush it out to me at the ranch.

We started to remake a picture called *Code of the West,* which had been done in the old days with Jack Holt and Evelyn Brent. The movie I was to make was only about three-quarters of a picture because the rest of it was stock stuff from the old picture. This is not a cop-out on my part, nor is it sour grapes. I didn't have enough experience with scripts, even though I had been an assistant director for a long time. My job had not been to worry about the story, my job had been to break the story down and prepare it for production. I wish I had had the experience then that I have now. I went ahead and shot this stuff.

They called me in one day and said, "We just signed a singer named Joe Morrison. His most famous song is 'Home on the Range.' So we're bringing him out here and putting him into your picture. We'll have him sing 'Home on the Range,' and change the title of the picture to that." It had nothing to do with that, but it was all right with me if that's what Paramount wanted, and I did it. The guy that produced it was a bully, a noisy guy, very insulting, and the kind of man I just couldn't get along with. I had a short fuse in those days. He called me down and said, "I don't like the way you've staged the song."

When the picture was finished, I didn't know whether it was good or not. We previewed it, and I remember the headline: "*Home on the Range* Won't Do." As you read the reviews, you found that they liked certain parts of it.

The one thing I had been told by this producer, Harold Hurley, was, "Don't worry about the reviews. These pictures are sold before they're made." The morning after the preview he called me into his office and the trade reviews were right on his desk. He said, "What do you say about that?"

I said, "You told me not to worry about them."

He said, "Artie, what kind of pictures do you want to make?"

I said, "I want to make a picture about a boy and a girl in the big city, the people I know and understand. What's with me and cowboys?"

He leaned over and pointed his finger right at my nose and said, "The trouble with you is you're too sensitive."

Then, because of an anti-Semitic slur, I hit him. I reached across the desk and hit him across his wrist. I said, "You know what you can do with your picture," turned and walked out of his office.

It didn't take long before the whole studio knew about it. About an hour later Henry Hathaway came up to me and said, "What happened between you and Hurley?"

I told him. Hathaway said, "Oh, you damn fool. He called you in there to rip you apart and give you another assignment as a director. But when you hit him —."

That was the end of my career as a director.

ATKINS: You mentioned that you were "Paramount-oriented." Wasn't that a feeling that almost everybody who worked at a studio had?

JACOBSON: Yes. You don't see it today because you don't work at one studio long enough. At the studio in those days we had a tremendous family. Everybody was out to make the best picture they could. There was no overtime, no nothing, only long, long hours of work. But we didn't care. It was fun, too, great fun.

I fell in love with a dancer on the lot. I worked all day, she worked all night, because most of the dance stuff was done at night. For two years, we courted on the front seat of a truck on the backlot.

ATKINS: I had heard that that sort of loyalty was more intense at Paramount.

JACOBSON: I doubt it very much. I think it was the same everywhere. We were so proud of our business. A couple of times I went to New York and one of my uncles said, "Is it true what happens in Hollywood? You meet a dame — " and so on.

I said, "Why don't you stop spreading words like that? It's disgusting." They couldn't understand why I felt that way, but I felt that our town was being besmirched. We were a very hard-working people. When you went out of town everybody thought you were having nothing but fun, sex, blah, blah. Oh, incidentally, some of the things they accused us of are true. We're no saints, you know.

ATKINS: You also said that you weren't prepared to direct.

JACOBSON: I found out later I was not prepared enough. I thought I was. That was my great trouble. I thought I was.

ATKINS: You'd been an assistant director for quite a long time. Are you saying that being an assistant director is not the best preparation for directing?

JACOBSON: Yes, I am, because being an assistant director has very little to do with creating a scene. The scene and the script are given to you. To be a good director, you have to be in on the writing of the script. After you get the script, if it needs rewriting, you need to be in on that. With an assistant director, it's the physical and technical things that count.

ATKINS: How about *A Farewell to Arms*?

JACOBSON: Frank Borzage was the director. We had Gary Cooper, Helen Hayes, and a woman named Mary Philips, who played Helen's girlfriend. Adolphe Menjou played the Italian officer.

ATKINS: Was there any location shooting on this film?

JACOBSON: No, we made the whole thing at the studio ranch.

ATKINS: By location I meant places like the ranch.

JACOBSON: In those days, they didn't go to Europe, but many years later Selznick remade it, and it was a bust. They only sent second units to Europe on very rare occasions. Nobody had that kind of money to spend. Then we got into process work, for backgrounds. Occasionally cameramen would go to Europe with certain assistants, and shoot the backgrounds.

ATKINS: Did you do that?

JACOBSON: Oh, yes, many times. I missed one that I wanted to do. I was called one time when I was freelancing, to go to Buenos Aires to do a background job for Selznick, with Cary Grant and Ingrid Bergman. I had to turn it down because I was already committed to something else.

There's a thing in *A Farewell to Arms* called the Italian retreat—a famous incident that actually happened during the war. It had to be done by a second unit, because Borzage didn't have the time to do it, and it was all at night in rain and mud. They hired an artist to sketch out all the scenes of the entire retreat. It was so impressive that they figured that they could surround him with all of us and have him put what he had drawn onto the screen. With our help, he directed the second unit, and it turned out fine.

As a result, he became a director. His name was Jean Negulesco. As you know he's a fine artist. He does everything, even single line drawings. He does some beautiful things.

The other thing about *A Farewell to Arms* is that Charles Lang invented a scene that was copied many, many times. Gary Cooper, a wounded soldier, is taken out of an ambulance, put on a gurney, and rolled down a hospital corridor. He's put in a bed, and as his head is lifted the door opens and he sees Helen Hayes, his sweetheart, come in, and she runs over and kisses him.

Charlie got this idea, and it worked beautifully. The camera took the place of his eyes. First you saw the sky. Then all you saw was the ceiling of the corridor and faces that went by and looked down at him. Then the camera moved over onto the bed, and Helen Hayes ran over and kissed the lens. It was very effective.

ATKINS: When a cameraman gets an idea like that, doesn't he have to have it okayed by the director?

JACOBSON: Oh, sure. The director has the final word. But a director looks forward to it. When a director has a cameraman who has imagination, he's a lucky man.

ATKINS: The logistics of a war picture must have been difficult.

JACOBSON: Again we get back to when you're laying it out. You look at the script and it says, "The Blues fight the Grays." That's only an eighth of a page in the script. Do you know what it means to put on the screen "The Blues fight the Grays"? You have to stage a war scene, and that takes three or four days.

One problem we had in the young days was when writers would write, "It is dusk or twilight." We had to go to them and say, "We can't photograph dusk or twilight. There's no such thing. Is it day or night?" Then we learned that there was what we called "the magic hour" — a thing called twilight. It couldn't be too dark, because then you wouldn't have enough exposure to photograph, but, just at a given time, especially if you had buildings with lights in them, and clouds in the sky and the sun in the right spot, you could get a shot. You had about twenty minutes. You'd go out an hour ahead of time and get all set up and rehearsed, and then stand there with your thumb on the camera button. Just when it was right, you'd do it.

ATKINS: Would such a thing work in Technicolor?

JACOBSON: Sure. The speed of the film is completely different, but the cameramen had gotten so much better by then.

ATKINS: Can you tell me about Billy Bitzer?

JACOBSON: Yes. He was famous because he had been Griffith's cameraman, and they had introduced the close-up. When they first used it, people would say, "What's that, a head bobbing around in the air?" When the film was put together they realized what it was.

He was offered a job for about three hundred fifty dollars, in the *Ziegfeld Follies.* They did a number called "My Lady's Lips," where the whole background was a pair of lady's lips that were moving.

Somebody got hold of Billy and offered him the job to film the background lips. Billy had hocked his camera, the time had expired, and he'd lost it. I knew Billy. I was always on his tail, because I wanted to work with him, and see how he did things. I told you that before I came to Hollywood I had my own camera. So I lent him my camera and went along with him as his assistant. My lens wasn't good enough, so he got a lens and taped it onto the camera. I think we worked eight days, and I got twenty-five dollars a day.

When the show opened, I was to meet him in the lobby of the theater and he would pay me. When he and his wife came out he was drunk. I asked her what had happened. She said that he had sat all through the show and had kept pulling a bottle out of his pocket. I never saw Billy again and I never got my two hundred dollars. He gave me a picture of himself, with a cigar. He even hand-tinted the red tip of the cigar. He wrote on it, "To Artie. He'll make it because he knows he doesn't know it all. Billy." I don't know where the picture is, but I have it someplace.

ATKINS: Do you know whether he received credit, say in the program of the *Follies,* for that?

JACOBSON: No. He might have. Billy Bitzer, God bless him, a wonderful guy, was a terrific drunk. That's why he lost out in the business.

ATKINS: There were many other films which you worked on during the early thirties, when the techniques of sound were becoming refined. One was *Too Much Harmony,* in 1933.

JACOBSON: They called our director, Edward Sutherland, "The Little Iron Man." He was never fatigued and always had fun. He was related in some way to Bill Le Baron, who was the operating head of the studio. Eddie made a lot of comedies, nothing spectacular, and a lot of knock-'em-out musicals. He was the director of the movie we were doing during the earthquake — *International House.*

ATKINS: You worked on *Good Dame* in 1934. Leon Shamroy was the cameraman.

JACOBSON: Marion Gering was the director. One night in the projection room he said to Schulberg, "After the rushes I'd like you to stay and see a few feet of film of my wife, Dorothy Le Baire. The cameraman went out and photographed these scenes without any equipment at all — no lights, no nothing."

They ran it and it was absolutely beautiful. Schulberg asked who did it. Gering said, "A man named Shamroy."

Nobody ever heard of him. Within a week Shamroy was under contract to B. P. Schulberg. As a result of that, of course, he photographed practically every picture that Sylvia Sidney did, because of the relationship between Schulberg and Sidney, and one of the pictures was *Good Dame.*

We had a group of stock kids, "The Golden Circle Kids." One was the Spider Woman, another the Tiger Woman, depending on the publicity department. Kathleen Burke was the Spider Woman. She was a black-haired, blue-eyed Irish girl. She'd lost her job long before *Good Dame,* when her option time came. She came to my office one day. She had a child and was stony broke, and she asked for a suggestion of where she could get a job.

It just happened that we had a scene in the picture that took place in a carnival, where a scantily dressed girl was holding a python. She had to tickle the python so that it stuck out its tongue, and the audience saw that it was real and alive. I asked Kathleen to do the scene. The studio was paying five hundred dollars, which in those days and even today, was a lot of money. She was terribly afraid of snakes, and at first she refused the job, but she was so desperate that she said she'd do it.

The next morning we set up the scene with three cameras, because there was only going to be one take. The director didn't want anything to do with the scene and told me to take over, which I did. Kathleen came on the set, and we rehearsed with a rubber snake, and I said to her, "You've got to stop shaking." She did the scene with the real snake, and I've never seen such courage. I made arrangements so that she could get paid that day, and that was the beginning and end of Kathleen Burke.

I heard on television that Sylvia Sidney was going to be on some program and that she was going to talk about her eye surgery. In *Madame Butterfly,* they pulled back and stuck tape on the corner of her eyes to make her look Japanese. It pulled the skin away, and in order to keep shooting they covered the skin with medication and makeup. By the time the picture was finished her skin was very sore, and I wouldn't be a bit surprised if that had affected her in later years. People got what they called "make-up poisoning." With make-up poisoning, your skin couldn't breathe. They put that make-up on pretty thick in the old days. Everybody in the silent pictures looked like they had jaundice, from a yellowish make-up. Then if you used panchromatic film you used a different color make-up which was sensitive to red. Today they don't use very much make-up, and what they do use is so sophisticated that it's very fine.

We had Klieg eyes, too. They used to warn you not to look into the Klieg lights, because it would burn the surface of your eye. Many times they had to put raw potato peelings on your eyes and make you sit in a dark room for a couple of days. It was horrible.

ATKINS: The next film I wanted to ask about is *The Big Broadcast of 1936.*

JACOBSON: We did that in 1935, with Norman Taurog. It took forever. In the cast were Jack Oakie, Akim Tamiroff, Lyda Roberti, and Wendy Barrie. Nat Finston was the music director. The story was that George Burns and Gracie Allen were selling a television set that was inside a suitcase.

When the picture was finished there was no picture. It was a lemon. Barney Glaser came up with the idea that to save the picture we'd find the best acts we could, put them on that television thing, and when the picture started to sag, cut to that.

They signed up Ray Noble and his Orchestra, who in those days were *it.* We got Amos 'n' Andy, and Fox and Walters, a great dance team. Walters became Charles Walters, the director at MGM. Jessica Dragonette was in it.

In order for us to do this, we all had to go to New York. Those people could not leave their jobs and fly out here. We made arrangements to meet Amos 'n' Andy in Chicago between trains, and sent the unit manager on ahead. Unfortunately he was the kind of unit manager who spent the week in New York and shacked up with somebody.

We got there on a Saturday morning and were supposed to shoot Monday morning at the Long Island Studio. The first thing we were going to do would be the simplest: a woman standing in front of nothing, singing a song.

The song was already pre-recorded by Jessica Dragonette — "Alice Blue Gown," and Taurog had said he wanted somebody to get with the person who made her clothes and have a soft blue dress made, one we could put a little breeze on, so it would blow. The only thing the unit manager hadn't attended to was the dress.

We all went to Jessica Dragonette's apartment Saturday afternoon. Nat Finston went with us. Taurog showed up in a tuxedo, because he had a date with his wife and some people. Miss Dragonette was there with her sister, who was a gofer. If you wanted anything from Jessica you did it through her sister.

Taurog asked to see Miss Dragonette's clothes, so we could choose what she would wear in the picture. The sister brought out about twelve dresses and hung them around the living room. Taurog kept looking at his watch, and finally decided on a certain skirt and a certain bodice, if it were powder blue. And with that he disappeared, saying, "I'll see you Monday morning on the set."

Everyone else went, too and left me standing there. I said to Dragonette, "It's Saturday evening. Everything is closed up tight until Monday morning. Who makes your clothes?"

She told me, Mary Paul, and we went up to Miss Paul's apartment on 86th Street. I told Miss Paul the situation, and she said she could make the powder blue skirt and bodice.

"How long do you think it would take?"

She said, "Six weeks. When do you need it?"

"Monday morning." There was a long silence. But she said she would try to do it. She phoned all her workers, who assembled, and it was like a Disney scene, as they started to work. They found enough material, had it dyed and dried, and were working. We got Dragonette down there for one fitting.

Sunday afternoon I got a call from Norman Taurog. "How's it going?"

"Fine."

"Well, I got a thought. Dragonette's hair is too long. I'd like her hair about two inches shorter. See you tomorrow."

I got hold of Eddie Senz, the biggest faker in the world. He's made a fortune, with the moustache and the smock and the crap that goes with it. He's just another make-up man, another hairdresser. I took Jessica to his shop. While we were there the phone rang. It was Norman. He said he'd like her hair two shades lighter.

The next morning I had Miss Dragonette in the studio at seven o'clock, with Mary Paul and Eddie Senz. At five minutes to nine she was on the set, ready to shoot. Taurog looked at her and said, "Fine. What was the big deal?" But here's the topper: when we got back to Hollywood they cut the picture — and the one thing they cut out was the number with Jessica Dragonette.

I think it had cost the studio about three thousand dollars, which was a lot in those days. The unit manager, who should have taken care of all this, had to explain to the studio why he hadn't.

Ray Noble and his orchestra were playing at the Rainbow Room in New York. We gave them a nine o'clock call, and it was going to take two days to shoot their stuff.

At three o'clock in the afternoon they packed up. I asked the manager of the band where they were going.

He said, "We're going back to get ready to do the show tonight."

"But you're supposed to be here until six." I called Lou Diamond, the head of Paramount music in New York.

He said, "Didn't anybody tell you they were only going to work until three?"

Taurog asked me what was happening and when I told him, he said, "That's the way they do it here." New York was no help at all.

ATKINS: Wasn't there quite a rivalry between Paramount in Hollywood and New York?

JACOBSON: Yes. Wanger was the head of the New York studio. Whenever Schulberg came to New York they used to put his picture up on the wall. A lot of the people had their homes furnished from the studio. They'd rent stuff for a set and never send it back. They'd send it to their homes.

ATKINS: Did that ever happen in Hollywood?

JACOBSON: Not to my knowledge.

ATKINS: You mentioned that Paramount had relinquished the ownership of the Astoria Studio.

JACOBSON: Oh, yes. They had closed that up a long time before. Within three months after I left, they padlocked the studio, and just closed it down. The Paramount releases of 1932 were all made in 1931. Walter Wanger, who was the head of the studio came out here, and became an independent producer.

ATKINS: That same year you were back in Hollywood, and you worked on a movie called *F-Man.*

JACOBSON; Jack Haley had a contract to finish. He had one picture left. They decided in order to finish out the contract they'd make a quick comedy. The producer said, "And don't take over twelve days. We don't want to put any money in it."

Somebody came up with the idea to make a picture about an F-Man, a dope who's not good enough to be a G-Man. They had a director floating around who did the old Hal Roach comedies, Edward Cline, a very nice guy, who had been a big director.

I went to the bathroom one day, and when I came back they were taking down the set. I said to Cline, "We've got another scene to do on this set, a closeup of Jack Haley."

He said, "We're moving to the backlot. We'll do it there. Who the hell will know the difference?"

That's the way they made that picture. I remember the girl in it. She became a character actress, Adrienne Marden. Those pictures were what you called the fill-ins. When you weren't doing a big picture you did one of these. That's why you worked 365 days a year. You always worked.

ATKINS: Who were the directors who would let you direct?

JACOBSON: Well, people who became your friends like Wesley Ruggles. He let me do things like direct second units, and it was the same with George Seaton. As a result of working with Wesley, I was promoted to head of talent.

Directors

ATKINS: You worked with many directors. Was your function pretty much the same with each one?

JACOBSON: Not necessarily. It all depended on how much the director wanted of you. Sometimes I worked with weak directors who were very dependent. They'd say, "You do it," which I liked to do. Strong directors said, "Look, don't take over." Each director had his own idea of what the assistant director should do.

I'll give you an idea of how it worked. I was assigned to a director who was known to be tough but fair, Wesley Ruggles. He was getting ready to do a picture with Ben Bernie, Jack Oakie, and Dorothy Dell, called *Shoot the Works*. I was very pleased that the studio thought enough of me to assign me to Ruggles, who was his own producer/director. He was *it*. When he was *it*, I was *it*, too. I felt looked up to.

The first scene was to be in the Lower East Side of New York, and it was to look cheap and sleazy. We were going to use about a hundred fifty extras. I was tickled silly because I was born and brought up in that neighborhood and knew it like the palm of my hand. I was able to tell the wardrobe people what to do, and the prop men what to get.

The first morning of work I took my guts in my hands and said to the great Wesley Ruggles, "Mr. Ruggles, do me a favor. You know, the first half hour on a set with a lot of extras is turmoil. Instead of coming in at eight o'clock, please don't come in until 8:30. By 8:30 I'll have it completely organized, and quieted down, and I'll be able to devote myself to you."

"You got it." That's the way he was. Any time he wanted to talk to you he called you over and you got down on your haunches and nobody else could hear what he had to say to you.

The next morning, my first with this big director, I was a little nervous. At eight o'clock I started getting these people all ready. He didn't live up to what he promised to do. I could feel him come in the door. When you're in the picture business as long as I've been, you see out of the corner of your eye. You sense everything. I went right along with my work, and at 8:30 I turned around and said, "Good morning. I'm ready to rehearse it for you."

He said, "Go ahead." I was pleased with it, but he said, "Cut it. Cut it." I was worried. He sat there, with his pipe, with argyle socks that were falling down, and his feet up on the tripod. He was pulling his hair straight up and I learned later that when he was doing that he was annoyed. He called me over, and I leaned down.

He said, "How long will it take you to replace all these people?" He talked about changing the wardrobe and all that business. "It's not right."

I said, "Until at least one o'clock."

He said, "Do it."

I started to walk away, but then I came back and said, "Mr. Ruggles, change them to what? What's wrong?"

He said, "The atmosphere, the people, they don't look — ."

I said, "Mr. Ruggles, I'm very pleased to be working with you, but when I get all through, I may not be working with you. You see all these people, the kid and the woman with the shawl and the old man with the yarmulka on? That's me and my sister and my grandfather!

I was born and brought up here. I know these people. You might not like it because it's not what you saw in your mind's eye, but don't tell me it's wrong, because it's as right as anything could be." My heart pounded. I waited.

There was a long silence, and then he turned around to the cameraman, Leo Tover. He said, "Leo, are you ready?" Leo said, "Any time." He turned to me and said, "Let's go. Let's shoot it."

ATKINS: *I Met Him in Paris* was another Wesley Ruggles film.

JACOBSON: Claudette Colbert, Robert Young, Melvyn Douglas and Lee Bowman were in that. Melvyn Douglas was wonderful. Bob Young got to be one of my dearest friends.

ATKINS: How did you and Claudette Colbert get along?

JACOBSON: She and I did not get along at the beginning, and then we got to be friends. I'll bet Claudette still has the first nickel she ever made. She lives in Barbados or someplace like that. She was very much in love with Dr. Jack Pressman, I must say. She was a hypochondriac. By the time we got through with the forty-nine days in Sun Valley, he had been up there twenty-five of them. Every time she sneezed he came up and brought half his equipment. It was in her hotel suite.

I had worked with her before. In 1930, when I was in New York, we did a picture called *Young Man of Manhattan.* I didn't want to stay there after *Royal Family,* but I was stuck. I had Freddie Spencer, who was Walter Wanger's college friend, as my assistant. I was very careful about what I asked him to do, because I did it over again by myself.

Claudette was queen of all she surveyed, which did not impress me — I was there to do a picture. There was one day when I had told Claudette personally that she was to go up to her dressing room and come back after lunch and do one more scene in her present costume with her hair up. When lunch was over I said to Freddie, "Where is Claudette?"

He didn't know, but he went to get her. She came in with her hair down, in a nightgown.

I said to her, "Claudette, there's a horrible mistake. I told you not to change."

She said, "You did not."

I said, "Freddie, you were standing right there," and with that Freddie turned and ran, scared. She was overpowering. I repeated, "I did tell you not to change," and she said, "You're a liar."

Well, that's all I needed. My hair went straight up, and I said, "Don't you ever call me a liar, you bitch. Who the hell do you think you're talking to? You can be Queen down here with all these guys, but don't you ever talk to me like that."

With that, she ran to Wanger's office, with me right on her heels. When we got to Wanger's office, there was a rail with a little gate. I beat her to it, and opened the gate. I said, "You go in first, and be careful what you say because you're going to be sorry if you don't tell the truth."

With that we were both in Wanger's office and she screamed, "Get him the hell off this picture. If you don't, I'm going to get off."

I said, "Walter, get me off the picture. Send me back to Hollywood. It's disgusting to have to work like this, ridiculous."

I explained the whole thing, and he said, "I believe you, Artie. But why don't you simmer down and both go back to work."

I said, "I'll go back to work on one condition: that for the rest of the picture I don't have to talk to this woman." I said that right in front of her. That's the way we finished the picture.

Later, we were back in Hollywood, and for three years we passed each other on the lot as if we didn't exist. But I was always sort of a trouble-shooter on the lot, and one day Sam Jaffe asked me to go down to the set of *Three-Cornered Moon,* and help straighten something out about fifteen taxis. It was an outdoors set, and the cast and crew were all having lunch on the lawn of this mansion. Claudette was sitting there, and when I got out of the studio car she said, "What the hell are you doing here?"

I said, "Excuse me," and turned to Elliott Nugent and said, "What's your problem?"

I straightened out the problem with the taxis, and I went back to where she and Nugent were standing. I said I'd stick around for a while to make sure everything was all right.

She said, "I've got something to say to you."

I said, "Whatever you have to say to me will keep. Forget it."

She said, "No. You've really got nuts, haven't you?"

I said, "Yes, I've got nuts. Any objection?"

She said, "Will you shake hands with me?"

I said, "Yes, I'll shake hands with you. What the hell have I got to lose?"

She looked at me and said, "You son-of-a-bitch," and we were friends from there on.

I wouldn't put up with those people. By the same token I was in love with Carole Lombard. I'd kiss her feet, because she was such a wonderful person. Irene Dunne, the same. Great people.

We also used a technical director on *I Met Him in Paris.* I said to him, "Did you ever act?"

He said, "I did in Germany." We made him a hotel clerk. That was Fritz Feld, and he was a hotel clerk from there on.

We found the location for that picture at Sun Valley, which wasn't open to the public yet. We found a beautiful spot to build St. Moritz, but it was twelve miles from the lodge. We built a whole hotel front that they matched with photographs of St. Moritz. We built the entire set, ice rink and all. The weather was so changeable. At four o'clock in the morning it was sometimes below zero, sometimes thirty-two above. By six o'clock it was forty-five. By noon it was eighty, and then it would go back down again. That's why everybody caught cold. During that one hour, at noon, everybody stripped to the waist and skied. Our great trouble was to keep the ice from melting on the skating rink during that two hours at noontime. When it got hot, the ice got slushy. There was a lot of skating stuff in the picture.

We had blizzards that took the roof right off of our shack, and the weather was so crazy that every morning we had to send a snow plow from the hotel to the set, and also one from the set to the hotel, so that we could get through. We went to the set eighteen days and we were there forty-nine, so you can imagine the things that must have gone wrong, but we got a good picture out of it.

The place was built, developed, and owned by W. Averell Harriman, and he was up there at the time. He got very interested in what we were doing. To us it was hard work, but there was something about making movies that was glamorous to everybody else.

Harriman brought these beautiful girls up, too, for publicity purposes. They could be swimming in the hotel pool with the snow all around them in the middle of the day. I didn't want them to get mixed up with our workers. Since there wasn't enough room to start with, we put our workers in a hotel twelve miles away, in a town called Ensley, and put an assistant director with them. We ran six cars up on the railroad spur, and they all had drawing rooms. With the cast and crew in the hotel we had enough room. There were two hundred sixteen people.

One day the boys from the train came to me and said that they were charging them twenty-five cents for a Coke in the diner. Coke in those days was a nickel.

I went to some man and said, "Who do I talk to about this?"

He said that the man in charge was in Salt Lake City. With that, Mr. Harriman came over and sat down with us. He said, "How's everything going, Artie?" By this time it was "Artie." I had ingratiated myself as much as I could because I knew we were going to need an awful lot of things. We had a unit manager who was afraid of his own shadow, and he was afraid to talk to Mr. Harriman.

I said, "It's not going good. I've got a revolution on my hands. Your men down at the spur charged our grips twenty-five cents for a Coke, and one of the boys said that's un-American.

He said, "Don't worry about it." From then on, for forty-nine days, nobody ever paid for a Coke.

Another time, one of our girls came to me and said, "We want to go home. The place and the food down there is just horrible."

I said I'd see what I could do. Without telling anyone who we were, Mel Epstein, who was my assistant, and I went down and ate there. Sure enough, the food was vile. I went into the kitchen, and it was just awful, with grease everywhere. The woman who owned this hotel was leasing it to Union Pacific Railroad. Salesmen stopped there, and they didn't give a damn, but these girls were used to better things.

I went to Mr. Harriman, and said, "I've got a problem." He had the entire kitchen gutted, refurbished it, and put Union Pacific cooks and waiters in there. From then on, we ate there.

There came a wonderful day when we were doing a thing called skijoring. It's just like water-skiing on skis, except that instead of a boat you use a team of horses along a road. We photographed it by preceding them on a fast-moving sled, with great mounds of snow on either side of the road. I happened to look around forward, and there, coming flat-out like a bat out of hell, was Mr. Harriman. He had three cameras on him and was photographing us. I knew that it wasn't going to be long before he'd have to step out of the way or we'd run him down, and as we passed we'd see him in the background and it would ruin the shot. I had a megaphone with me, and yelled, "Get off the road and stay out of the shot."

Sure enough, we went by and there was no Harriman. He had dived into the nearest snowbank, cameras and all, and disappeared. From then on he was my assistant, and he went out with us every day. He helped serve the lunch. We had a ball, and got to be great friends.

ATKINS: I presume they had doubles for the stars?

JACOBSON: Oh, yes. We used the kitchen help. We had wigs and so on.

ATKINS: How soon after the picture was shot did the Lodge officially open?

JACOBSON: Within a week after we finished. As a matter of fact, there were quite a few people who came in long before. One of them was Gloria Vanderbilt. She was just a kid then.

Another thing about Sun Valley: we had a grip, Tommy Hadley, who operated the big crane. Ruggles said, "I want the crane up there." So they dismantled the crane in Hollywood, put it on a flatcar, and took the whole thing up to Sun Valley. They re-assembled it, and used it just like we were on a stage. When Ruggles wanted something, Ruggles got it.

ATKINS: Did the studio or Sun Valley do any publicity tie-ins when the picture opened?

JACOBSON: Frankly, I just don't remember. The big publicity thing at Sun Valley was skiing stripped to the waist.

In 1939, Wesley Ruggles directed a picture called *Invitation to Happiness,* with Fred MacMurray and Irene Dunne. I had just been promoted, and the assistant director was Mel Epstein. Ruggles sent me to New York with a cameraman, because the writer, Claude Binyon, had dreamed up a sequence that took place in New York. The night before MacMurray's big fight, he would sit on a bench on Riverside Drive. Across the Palisades, where the lights are, he would see the form of a sleeping woman in his mind's eye, and he would be relaxed and ready for the fight.

Ruggles said to me, "Go shoot me the sleeping woman." It was July in New York, and hot. I tried to find the sleeping lady, but there was no such thing. I called Ruggles in Hollywood and told him. Ruggles said, "Well, stick around and keep looking. Claude is sitting right here with me, and he says he saw it once. If he saw it, you can find it."

We made some beautiful shots of the ferryboats going across the Hudson at night, and I kept calling Ruggles every night to tell him we hadn't found the sleeping woman. Finally I asked him to send Claude to New York to help us find it, and he did. At that time, Claude weighed about 270 pounds. When he got to New York on a July night, with that heat, he took one look and said, "Well, I guess it's not there anymore," and we all went home.

We did the shots at Paramount in the trick department. But I had a wonderful time in New York, and that's the way Ruggles was. He let me do that.

ATKINS: You did several other pictures with Wesley Ruggles before this, including *The Bride Comes Home.*

JACOBSON: There was a unit. Wesley Ruggles was the boss — the producer/director. I was the assistant director and assistant producer. He gave me that title. Nearly everything Ruggles did was written by Claude Binyon. Otho Lovering was the cutter. Leo Tover was the cameraman. There was also a secretary.

The Bride Comes Home was a story about a girl, Claudette Colbert, who had been very rich and had become poor. She got a job on a men's magazine run by Fred MacMurray, and this couple eventually fell in love. There were a lot of very good light comedy scenes.

We made a lot of the picture in Chicago. Wesley Ruggles was the kind of a director who, when he wanted to show a couple in love and completely oblivious to their surroundings, found the busiest place imaginable to shoot the scene. The couple would just look into each other's eyes. In Chicago, they played the scene leaning on the rail right in the middle of the Michigan Link Bridge. Half of the background was Chicago and the other half was the lake.

He also wanted to do something at twilight because it was romantic. Dewey Wrigley was the process cameraman. We utilized the magic hour, where you really only had about twenty minutes, especially in summer. In Chicago in August it was light until nine o'clock in the evening, and by that time everybody had gone home, and all the buildings had no lights in them. Ruggles told me to get the thing set up so that there would be lights on and people around.

I went to Balaban and Katz, who were Paramount. They had a finger in the mayor's office. On Wacker Drive they had big Cleopatra's Needle lights with three big white bulbs. I made arrangements for them to get in touch with the superintendents of all the buildings and have them put on the lights on a given five nights. We had to do it five nights running because we had five different angles to shoot. The first night that we shot it, everybody in Chicago that belonged to the government turned out.

We were never bashful about asking for things, because we always got them. There's always money. We used about fifty off-duty cops, and they all got money. We found out that they changed shifts every four hours, so many more cops could get in on the gravy.

Just before we were going to do the first scene my assistant came running over to me and said, "We forgot one thing. You know that shot down Wacker Drive? They will not have their automobile headlights on."

We got the captain, and said, "String out the cops down Wacker Drive and yell to the drivers, 'Turn on your lights.'" That's the way we got the shot.

The cameraman said that the Cleopatra's Needle lights were not strong enough, and he wanted to put photo-flood bulbs in them. The Department of Power said that it couldn't be done — that the fuses would be blown. But you didn't say to Ruggles, "It can't be done." If you said, "It's going to take a month," he'd say, "All right. Take the month. But do it." We went back there at four o'clock one morning, and our electrician and grip from the studio shinnied up these poles, with a pocketful of bulbs. They changed the bulbs, and it worked fine. When the cops came along, and asked what we were doing, we slipped them some money and they didn't bother us. But how were we going to explain this to the Department of Power? We got hold of the liaison man, and we gave the head of the Power Department a beautiful gift.

There was no such thing as "it can't be done." If you said that three or four times, you were looking for work.

We started to do another picture with Wesley Ruggles called *La Chienne.* We had a wonderful cast: Carole Lombard, Cary Grant, Charlie Ruggles. We never completed it, but it was finally made as *The Woman in the Window.*

It was based on a book. He had me break it down and send the breakdowns to Paris. That's why I became his assistant producer. He had a still cameraman sent out to every street corner that was mentioned in the book, and photograph them in such a way that you could see the names of the streets on the lamp-posts. He said, "Try it this way, and if it's no good, you go on over there yourself and do it." There was no such thing as "it's too far."

I was with him for about seven glorious years, and I loved him. The chair I'm sitting in was his. The lighter and that box with the pennies in it — those were his. I revered him, and he made some great pictures.

ATKINS: Do you recall *Rich Man's Folly*?

JACOBSON: Nothing special there except that John Cromwell directed it. I had worked with him before on *Street of Chance,* with William Powell and Jean Arthur. Powell played the famous gambler, Abe Rothstein.

ATKINS: My credits show that John Cromwell played a part in *Street of Chance.*

JACOBSON: He may have played a bit, but I don't remember it.

ATKINS: How did you like working with him?

JACOBSON: Oh, I loved him. I had such respect for him. You see, strange things happened in those days. John Cromwell was in a play in downtown Los Angeles. Somebody said they had seen the play and that there was an actor in it, a tall angular man, who did an outstanding job. They were so hungry for actors that they brought him to the studio and gave him a contract as actor, writer, and director. The first thing he did was a small acting part in a picture. He played a detective, who's supposedly a telephone repairman. In the rushes, Schulberg fell in love with this: you saw Cromwell come in, in the background, kneel down at the baseboard, and, in the middle of the scene, all of a sudden he took his handkerchief out and blew his nose. Schulberg said it was the greatest piece of acting he'd ever seen. He didn't know whether it was the director or Cromwell himself who'd done it. So, Cromwell immediately became a director.

He was a great research man. For instance, if we were going to do a courtroom scene, we used to go downtown and sit in the courtrooms for days, and get all the little bits of business, such as — whoever heard of it before — on the judge's bench there was an electric fan going, because it was hot. It was before air conditioning. All the time a man is being tried for his life, the clerk over there was on the telephone, maybe talking to a girlfriend. Who knows? He's whispering, of course. A guy came in and put a candy bar on somebody's desk and they started to eat it. Cromwell put these things in the picture. Everybody at the studio thought Cromwell was great.

ATKINS: Did *Street of Chance* have a courtroom scene?

JACOBSON: Yes, but there were others, also. There's one in *For the Defense,* where William Powell played William Fallon. William Powell came along when we went downtown. Cromwell insisted that Powell watch the way those attorneys worked.

There was a big defense attorney working, and they had a Negro on the stand who was the defendant in a murder trial. As we walked into the courtroom — of course arrangements were made in advance — the prosecuting attorney recognized Powell, turned to the jury and said, "Ladies and gentlemen of the jury, you may not believe in providence or coincidence, but I've been trying to tell you for days that this man is not telling the truth. And now if you'll turn around you'll see that one of our most famous actors, William Powell, just entered the courtroom. He doesn't look like an actor, does he? But let's go back to our defendant. I told you he was lying. He's acting. That's all he's doing, acting."

Whether or not that helped the defendant I don't know, but Powell got very embarrassed. We stayed and watched the trial, anyway. That's the way Cromwell used to work.

He's gone now, rest his soul. But he was a wonderful man. I saw him for the last time at the Guild tribute when he was an old, old man. I loved working with him because he understood actors.

A lot of movie directors just didn't understand actors, didn't want to. Joe von Sternberg said, "As far as I'm concerned they are clay. I break them down into a blob of clay and then I mold them."

Well, when actors heard that! I think Hitchcock said they were only cattle.

ATKINS: He later said he was only kidding.

JACOBSON: But he said it. That's the important thing.

ATKINS: What about George Abbott and *The Sea God*?

JACOBSON: George Abbott was a big Broadway director and producer. He was coming from New York to do a picture and I was assigned to it.

The script I was given to read was ridiculous. It was about a man whose ship is destroyed while he is exploring the ocean floor. When he comes to the surface in his diving suit, the island natives think he is the sea god.

It was decided that we'd shoot on Catalina. In the cast were Richard Arlen, who played the sea god, Fay Wray, and Eugene Pallette.

We needed a lot of natives, who would be housed on Catalina for two weeks, so it was a job everybody wanted. They had to be able to swim because they were to be in outrigger canoes, and we wanted to be sure they could take care of themselves in case anything happened. We were using Negroes, and they all said they could swim. We also had several Hawaiians, who were lifeguards, in each boat.

I didn't want to take a chance, because in all the years I'd been around I'd never been responsible for an accident or anyone being hurt. At White's Landing, at the rear of Catalina, there's a pier. I told all the extras that I was going to test them by having them jump off the pier, and that if they couldn't swim, I would send them back. We all put on shorts, and to prove that there was no danger, I jumped in first.

Well, out of the hundred extras, we lost eighty, and we had to have more extras sent over.

We started to shoot a scene between the boy and girl, at the rail of the ship. George Abbott said to me, "Aren't we supposed to be five miles at sea in this scene? Are we five miles out?"

I said, "Oh, no, Mr. Abbott. But you don't have to go out that far. We're just shooting towards the horizon."

"But you'll get more of a roll out there."

I said, "You'll also get a lot of sick people. You may not even be able to shoot."

Abbott said, "When I wrote five miles at sea I meant five miles at sea," so we went out, and we had a hell of a day. Everybody got sick.

When we were going back, and were about an eighth of a mile from shore, Mr. Abbott peeled his pants off, jumped over the side of the boat, and swam in.

He was a tall, good-looking man who always looked very, very pale compared to all of us Californians. He and Henry King looked alike. As a matter of fact, one time when I was in New York, I met Abbott in the Paramount Building elevator. We rode down and walked to 50th Street, a six-block walk. By that time I realized I had been talking to Henry King. Abbott is a little older than Henry King.

ATKINS: How about *Sea Legs*, which was also shot on Catalina?

JACOBSON: That crazy thing. Victor Heerman, who was a comedy director, did that. In this picture, there was a French boat, so that all the sailors wore those blue berets with red pompoms. One of the big scenes was where they had to abandon ship, and fifty or seventy-five guys jumped overboard, with all these berets and pompoms.

ATKINS: Victor Heerman is another director who sort of disappeared.

JACOBSON: A lot of them did: Erle Kenton, Eddie Sutherland. This was because as the picture business went on, the stories got better. These guys who learned when talkies first started didn't know how to handle a story. But as far as shooting on Catalina is concerned, we shot there about twice a year. They were well equipped for us. You could move in there, and bring your equipment. But it wasn't Avalon. It was White's Landing, the tail-end of Catalina.

ATKINS: Did they have any film processing facilities there?

JACOBSON: No. But they had a special ferry service for motion picture people. We never looked at rushes, because the producer never came along. They'd phone in and tell you how the stuff was.

ATKINS: You worked on *Madame Butterfly*. How did they happen to do that as a non-musical?

JACOBSON: I don't know. Apparently Miss Sidney wanted to do it, and Cary Grant was under contract, so he played Pinkerton. It didn't set the world on fire. We had a Jewish Cho-Cho-San.

ATKINS: There was another all-star picture in 1932: *If I Had a Million*.

JACOBSON: I did three episodes on that, one with Lubitsch, one with James Cruze, and one with Norman McLeod. All you had to do was put Lubitsch's name in front of the theater and the people came in. He asked which one they wanted him to do, and they said, "You make it up yourself."

In the scene, about a hundred people were working in an office. They all looked alike, and were doing the same things, rote, rote. A messenger boy came in and walked away down to one of the desks and handed an envelope to Charles Laughton (he was under contract). The audience knew it was a check for a million dollars. He took off his eyeshade, got up, and walked to the office of the third vice president, then to the second vice president's office, and finally to the president's office.

The camera was on Laughton's back, but now it came around and he stuck out his tongue and gave the president big razzberry. That was Lubitsch. Well, that sequence swept the country. Everybody in the United States talked about it.

I worked on a sequence with Gene Raymond. The envelope was delivered to him just before he was to walk to the electric chair. As he was being dragged to the chair he was screaming, "I can get a lawyer," and then he was electrocuted. That was directed by Jimmy Cruze, who at one time had been a really big director and made some of the big silent pictures. He still dressed the way he did in the old days, with white duck pants, a white shirt, and a white cap. We all tried to help him in every way we could.

The other sequence was with W. C. Fields, which Norman McLeod directed. Fields was a man whose car was always getting bumped. When he got the check for a million dollars, he bought a car with a special bumper, and when a car came near him he knocked the car off the street.

I worked on one other sequence, with Charlie Ruggles. I can't remember who directed it. He was a little nebbish, and when he got his million dollars, he went into a crystal shop and broke every piece in the place.

It was a very successful picture, and later it became a television show.

ATKINS: What was W. C. Fields like in person?

JACOBSON: Oh, I loved him, and I loved working with him. He was a completely private person. Nobody could get near him. He liked me, and we got along fine.

Later he did a picture with Judith Allen, Jimmy Gleason and Gleason's partner, Bob Armstrong. We had a night scene where Fields put his hat on and walked out of his home. The exterior was in Pomona, where you see the door open, and we had matched it in the studio. On location, I went to the wardrobe man, and I said, "Where's his hat?"

He said, "I don't have it. He wore it home last night."

I told him he shouldn't have let Fields take it, or he should have had a duplicate hat. I went to Fields and told him that we needed the hat.

W. C. Fields said, "If anybody notices that I have a hat on in one scene and it doesn't match as I come out the door, then they're crazy, because when Fields is on the screen they look at me, not at my hat."

We called the studio, and they sent a car to Fields' house, all the way to Pomona, to get the hat. We skipped the scene until later.

Another thing about Fields was that he drank an awful lot and he had no respect or love for the front office. The front office was like a red flag in front of a bull. He had it in his contract that he always went home at six o'clock. We reached a point one night where, through some kind of mishap, we couldn't quite finish the day's work, which meant that we had to come back the next day. That would throw another company into chaos — because the idea was to take our set down that night and put their set up. The only way we could save it would be to work one hour after dinner, and because of unions and whatnot, you had to break for dinner.

Well, who was going to go and talk to W. C. Fields about coming back after dinner? This was unheard of. My boss, Sam Jaffe, came on the set, and said I should talk to Fields.

I went to him with tears in my eyes. He said, "Just one hour?"

I said, "If we're not through in an hour, you just walk."

About forty-five minutes into the dinner hour, when we were expecting everybody back in another fifteen minutes, Armstrong and Gleason came in. They were both drunk, and they were both in the scene with Fields. I was really worried. In ten minutes they started to laugh. It was a joke on me. They weren't drunk at all.

Then Bill came in. He always had a man with him who was a dresser or valet, and wore a white smock. This guy was carrying a saucer with an iced tea glass on it. The glass had a blotter on the top, so that nobody could tell what it was, but obviously it wasn't iced tea. I could tell that Bill had had a few, and I got worried again. I went to the prop man and we got a duplicate glass, put iced tea in it, and changed glasses.

We started rehearsing the scene. Bill picked up the glass, and took a drink. He turned and said, "What smart ass made that switch?" — and went home.

Fields never knew it was me. I felt badly about it, but that's that's the way it goes.

ATKINS: You worked on *Say It In French* and *Sing You Sinners* in 1938.

JACOBSON: *Say It In French* was made first. The director, Andrew L. Stone, went to the studio and said he could make a picture without sets. They called me in and assigned me to it, but I said to them before I even met him, "I don't understand this. How are you going to make a picture without sets? Is it all going to be on location?"

They said, "No, he says he can make it by going to New York with doubles and photographing all the backgrounds. Eventually he'll come back to Hollywood and shoot all the people against process backgrounds."

I said, "That makes sense."

I went and talked to him, and he said, "For instance, we'll work in the Waldorf-Astoria Hotel and we'll have people in the lobby go into the elevators."

I asked how he could do that. "You can't have the people walk up and push the elevator button on the background screen. You'll have to build a little piece of a set."

He said he knew a way around all the problems, but I said that it wasn't going to work. I told the studio, too, but they said, "If he says it's going to work, it will."

He was a friend of the head of the studio, so he went ahead. We did all this, and it never worked. We built sets.

ATKINS: How prevalent was process shooting in those days?

JACOBSON: It was very prevalent and successful. It took an awful lot of time, and it was only done when it was absolutely necessary for location. In this case, we photographed most of it in the Waldorf. We shot the Starlight Roof on the seventeenth floor. They had no electricity up there that we could use, so we dropped our cables seventeen stories down to generators on the sidewalk. The stuff we shot was beautiful.

We had some three hundred extras in evening dress. The officials of the Waldorf were invited to see the rushes, and they were so delighted that they moved my assistant and me from an ordinary room to a Louis XIV suite, where we stayed for thirty days. It was very nice.

There's a hotel off-Broadway called the Edison, that went right through from 46th Street to 47th Street. You went through revolving doors, down some steps, across the lobby and out the other doors.

In the story, we had a little racing car that had to get to the Queen Mary in eight minutes, through one-way streets. That was the chase, with a Western Union boy driving and the double for Ray Milland sitting in the back seat. The car drove through the doors, which were open, across the lobby, and out into 46th Street, then down Broadway against traffic, in and out to the riverfront, which is 12th Avenue. We had a thing where two freight cars were coupling up, and we drove through just before they did. Then the guy got off, ran up the gangplank, and jumped about five feet from the end of the gangplank, which was being moved down, onto the deck of the ship — with about a hundred feet below him.

ATKINS: Were you one of the people who arranged a chase like that?

JACOBSON: Oh, sure. It was a team effort. We had a unit manager who helped. This thing had to be done mathematically perfect. Otherwise that car would have been crushed between the two freight cars.

Andrew L. Stone is quite a mathematician, and we laid it out so that the freight cars were backing towards each other at a given slow rate of speed, which never varied. The doubles in the automobile went just so fast, and they under-cranked the camera to make the slowness normal. There was no chance of anyone being hurt, unless the engineer of either train or the kid driving didn't obey orders. Mathematically, there it was — at 50 miles per hour. To get a thrill, they had to do it so the paint was practically scraped off the car.

ATKINS: With modern motor-driven cameras, does the cameraman just set the film drive speed for the scene?

JACOBSON: Yes, but in the old days you had to do it by hand, under-cranking for fast speed and over-cranking for slow motion.

ATKINS: Did any of the cast of the film go East?

JACOBSON: No, just doubles. There was a little French actress in the picture, a dancer who specialized in cartwheels — Olympe Bradna.

They had Evelyn Keyes, but at the last minute they took her out and put in Irene Hervey. It was just another picture. They used some of the process stuff, but they had to build quite a few sets.

This was the only time I worked with Andrew L. Stone. We had one little run-in. He was so mathematically minded that everything he did was math.

For instance, when we went to the Rainbow Room with the three hundred extras, we had to shoot the backgrounds knowing what would be happening in the foregrounds with the principals. We had four different angles. He wanted me to give all the extras numbers so that when I called a number, the extras would do exactly the same thing in each cut.

I said that would embarrass me, that it wasn't necessary. He insisted on the numbers, so I said he'd better get himself another assistant director. But what I did, so that production wouldn't be held up — for Paramount's sake — was have my assistant, Holly Morse, handle the scenes. So Andy and I didn't hit it off so well after that.

I had a difficult time getting along with certain directors if I didn't respect their work. Many of those guys tried to shove it down your throat to show their authority.

ATKINS: Andrew L. Stone did a lot of pictures.

JACOBSON: Yes. You see, Andy used to do pictures independently, because he knew the trick of doing them for a price — cutting corners here and there. His wife did all the editing. So between them, they did all right.

ATKINS: The film's editor was Roy Stone, no relation.

JACOBSON: Yes. I did a lot of pictures with Roy.

Talent Department

ATKINS: I think that somewhere in this period you became head of the Paramount talent department.

JACOBSON: That was really as a result of Donald O'Connor and Ellen Drew. In 1936, we started to make *Sing You Sinners.* Wesley Ruggles was his own producer/director. He was a top man in the business, and I was very proud to be associated with him. The picture was with Bing Crosby, Mickey Rooney, and Fred MacMurray. At the last minute MGM took Mickey Rooney from us, because they had a picture they wanted to start right away with him, and they had the legal right to do it. That threw us into a spin. We had pre-recorded, were ready to shoot, and we didn't have the third brother.

Ruggles turned to me and said, "Find me another Mickey Rooney and we'll start the picture."

"What about the casting department?"

"Oh, the casting! You find him."

I said I'd try. As it happened, some friends of ours worked at MGM and my wife and I were invited to the annual party at the Biltmore Hotel. By the time we got to the party, I'd had quite a few drinks and I didn't know what town I was in. But I do remember that all through the party my wife kept poking me in the ribs with her elbow.

The next morning I asked her about it, and she said, "You know what you've been looking for all these weeks

— a Mickey Rooney? At the MGM party last night, they not only had a lot of the stars perform, but they hired a few extra acts to fill in. One act was called "The O'Connor Family." There was a lot of noise, and the curtains opened, and this kid slid right across the floor under your feet. He was about twelve years old; there's your Mickey Rooney."

I made contact with the agent, and Mrs. O'Connor and this kid came in. I hadn't told Ruggles about him yet. I asked him if he could act. He said, "If it's entertainment, I can do anything. I can sing, I can dance, I can act."

I took the records home that we had pre-recorded with Bing and Fred, and I had Donald come out to the house every night. By the end of the week, he not only knew every word of the script, he knew all the parts, and he was able to harmonize with Bing, on the records.

Now came the big moment of truth. Monday morning, when Ruggles got to his office, I brought Donald in and introduced him. Ruggles was a very stern looking man, with lines in his forehead and his cheeks. I introduced them, and Donald started to read some scenes. When the time came for the music, I turned it on. Ruggles caught on immediately. After about an hour, he told Donald to wait in my office across the hall.

We sat for about five minutes, and my heart was pounding. Then Ruggles said, "You know what's going to happen? While we're sitting here, someone's going to grab that kid. Get his name on a contract."

I explained that the casting department wouldn't listen to me, so he called Fred Datig and said he wanted Donald. That was the beginning of Donald O'Connor.

ATKINS: Donald O'Connor played a "fresh kid" in that film. Was he like that off-screen?

JACOBSON: No, just the opposite.

ATKINS: Did you have any problems as far as doing playbacks were concerned?

JACOBSON: None whatsoever. From the day he was born he was a professional, and he is to this day. He was twelve going on sixty, a completely thorough vaudevillian.

For example, I said, "Can you ride a race horse?"

He said, "No, but I'll learn," which he did.

In the race sequence he was the jockey. We used a double for Donald, but Wesley Ruggles was a perfectionist, and he said, "We have to see Donnie riding a little."

Donnie couldn't handle a race horse in a race — you'd take a chance of killing him. They made a hairpiece just like Donald's hair, and a mask just like Donald's face. It was made out of very fine rubber, with slits in the eyes and the mouth, and it slipped over the stunt double's head down into his collar. The race ran about seven minutes, and was shot at the Pomona fairgrounds. In many shots you saw the horses come towards you, and Donald's horse and rider came right up into the camera. It worked beautifully.

Donald was fun, and had a great sense of humor. Everybody loved him because he was such a pro. Bing fell in love with him too. They sang "Small Fry" together, and it became a tremendous hit. Of course *Sing You Sinners* was a hit.

We also had a girl named Terry Ray under a stock contract for seventy-five bucks a week. I thought that she'd be right for it. She wasn't the most experienced actress in the world, but Wesley Ruggles was a hell of a director. I went to Wesley and suggested that he use her.

He said, "Just bring her in when we're going to do something on film, so I can hear her tone of voice, and we'll go from there.

He liked her very much, but he said, "There's only one other person who has to like her: Bing. It's in his contract that he has to approve, but I'm sure there'll be no problem. You have to take her to Bing to be okayed officially."

I told her the story. She was very nervous. Bing was pre-recording on Stage 1, the recording stage. My office was in the building next to it. I told her to wait on the steps while I went in to talk to Bing. When I told him about the girl, he said, "If you and Wesley Ruggles approve, that's fine with me." He didn't want to see her.

I said, "I think that since you're being so nice about it, you deserve the pleasure of seeing what will happen in her eyes when you tell her that she's got the job."

I went outside and took her into the stage. When Bing finished his number I said, "Bing, I want you to meet Terry Ray."

He turned around and said, "How do you do?" He had no idea what was happening.

I said, "Bing, will you tell this little lady something? Just say these words, 'You have the job.'"

He said, "You have the job," and she fainted. She became Ellen Drew.

The man who was running the talent department, whose name I can't remember, had gone around the country looking for talent, and making tests. There was too much talk about his screwing around with the dames, so they fired him, just at the time that the picture came into the projection room, finished. One executive asked Ruggles where he had found Donald O'Connor and the girl who was in the picture, Ellen Drew.

Ruggles said, "Ask my assistant. He found them."

The studio offered me the talent department job, and Ruggles said, "I'll only let him go on one condition: that he replaces himself with someone like himself."

A friend of mine, Mel Epstein, was there, Ruggles accepted him, and I got the job.

ATKINS: What did you do as head of new talent?

JACOBSON: I had one assistant and two secretaries. The job was to find new talent, and once I found it and convinced certain people at the studio they should be put under contract for at least six months, it was my job to develop them, personally. It was also my job to become their agent inside the studio. I had to sell their services out to producers and directors.

I had a little workshop, where, if I felt somebody had potential, I would train them, and work with them. I'd work through a plate glass where they couldn't see me but I could see them and hear them. They could hear me when I pressed a button.

An agent came to see me, and said, "I have a girl who is going back to New York because she's up to here with Hollywood, but I think she's got something."

I told him to bring her in for a test, and he did. Her name was Edythe Marrener. I finally got Mr. Freeman to okay a contract for this gal, but I said to him, "I'm not going to let anybody see her until she's ready. When she's ready, she's going to start out with a lead. No fooling around with bits here and there — she doesn't need it."

One day, after I had been working with her for about two months, Joseph Youngerman came up to me in the commissary. He's one of my dearest friends, and at that time was William Wellman's assistant. He said, "You know, we're going to do *Beau Geste*. We can't find a gal to play the young girl in it, and Wellman told me to talk to you because he understands you've got yourself a bit of dynamite back there."

I said, "Joe, it's a nothing part. You'll ruin all the work I've done. So please tell him to forget it."

I went back to work. Right in the middle of the next bit of work, the door opened behind me in the dark, and Wellman came in, without my knowing who it was. All of a sudden he snapped on the lights, and said, "I want that girl."

She didn't know what the hell was going on. She couldn't even hear it. I said, "Please, no."

With that he hotfooted it to Le Baron's office, with me behind him. Wellman was a lot stronger than I was, so he got her. That was the first thing she did at Paramount, but I must say, from there on she went. She became Susan Hayward.

My assistant came to me and said, "I went to the Pasadena Playhouse last night, and I sat in the first row. When I went backstage, I must say I was fooled. I saw this seventy-year-old man taking his make-up off, and he's a twenty-year-old kid."

I told him to bring in the kid. His name was Bill Beedle and he said, "Oh, I don't need this business. I just did that for fun."

I made a test of him. The test found its way over to Columbia. Mr. Freeman called me in, and said that Harry Cohn wanted to buy half the kid's contract, and give him the lead in a picture. That was the beginning of *Golden Boy*, and William Holden.

ATKINS: Did you also scout for new talent outside the studio?

JACOBSON: Yes. I had an assistant named Milt Lewis. He was not married, so he had the night assignments. Every night of his life, seven nights a week, he was somewhere. He was the one who told me about seeing Bill Holden at the Pasadena Playhouse.

When I went to New York I saw eight shows a week. During the day, I'd have open house for all the agents in New York and tell them, "Bring anybody, even if you have had them up here before."

They had a talent scout there named Boris Kaplan. I saw many, many people.

I had worked on a picture with Ben Bernie. At this time he was playing at the Pennsylvania Hotel, and his brother was his agent, and also the agent for many acts. He said, "I know a lot of people."

I said, "I'll see them all. I can stay in New York as long as I have to."

He told me that he and Ben had made arrangements with the hotel for me to see a lot of acts in the room where he played, after they closed. Ben asked his boys to stay and play for all these young actors, and a group of them said they would. I was there all night long, they put on a show for me, but I never found one soul. It was great for Ben and his brother, and it gave all the actors a boost.

The only thing that came out of that trip to New York was Brenda Marshall, and Mary Martin, who was a star on Broadway. Nobody would touch her out here.

Mary used to sing a trick song called "Cara Nome," in which she would sing a falsetto, and then, while she was holding the falsetto she would rhythmize and dirty it down. She couldn't really sing that high, but it became very sensual and very sexual, and was a very entertaining bit of music. I made a test.

Andrew L. Stone was casting *The Great Victor Herbert*, with Allan Jones and a girl. When I brought the test back here I let all the producers see it, and he came running into my office. He said, "Artie, you've found my girl for *The Great Victor Herbert*."

I said, "Oh, the 'Cara Nome' thing. You're making a mistake — ."

He said, "Oh, she can do it. Don't tell me I'm making a mistake. I can feel it."

He went to Le Baron and got the okay to go to New York. He met Mary Martin, and she auditioned for him. He called me on the phone and said, "What have you done to me? She can't sing this."

I said, "I tried to tell you, but you wouldn't listen."

He said he was going to try it. He got a voice coach. She had to sing "Kiss Me Again." Well, that's really asking for it, but he finally did the picture with Mary.

In a way I was more or less responsible for Mary being back in Hollywood, even though everybody said they couldn't use her. Harry Cohn said she had an undershot jaw. He also said that Gene Tierney had a crooked mouth.

Talent searching was a matter of personal opinion and taste. One person could see something in someone and nobody else could. For instance, when I first released the test of Bill Holden to our studio, I insisted that the producers send me reports of their opinions before anyone outside saw it.

Arthur Hornblow, who was one of the bigwigs, said, "How can you waste your money making tests of this kid? He's got fishy eyes and an underslung jaw." He also sent me a note about Bob Messervey, saying, "Why do you test truck drivers?" It was Robert Preston. He came up with Constance Keane, who became Veronica Lake.

If you listened to the producers you'd never sign anybody except their friends. When I got in there they had a thing called the Golden Circle. It was a very sad job because I had to weed some of them out, as they had gotten contracts because they were friends of somebody. I was a hard-nosed guy, and said, "Look, there's no use your wasting time —."

ATKINS: At the time we're talking about, did all the studios have talent departments, and did they all send people East?

JACOBSON: Yes, yes. Not only East, but all over the country. If someone called and told me about a college show at a university, I'd go. Sometimes I found nothing, but you never could tell. You had to follow will-o'-the-

The young Arthur Jacobson with an even younger Clara Bow. Circa 1920.

The Scarecrow on location in Deerfield, Massachusetts. Jacobson far right, director Frank Tuttle, wearing cap, left of the camera. This Pathé production starred Glenn Hunter and Mary Astor. Circa 1920.

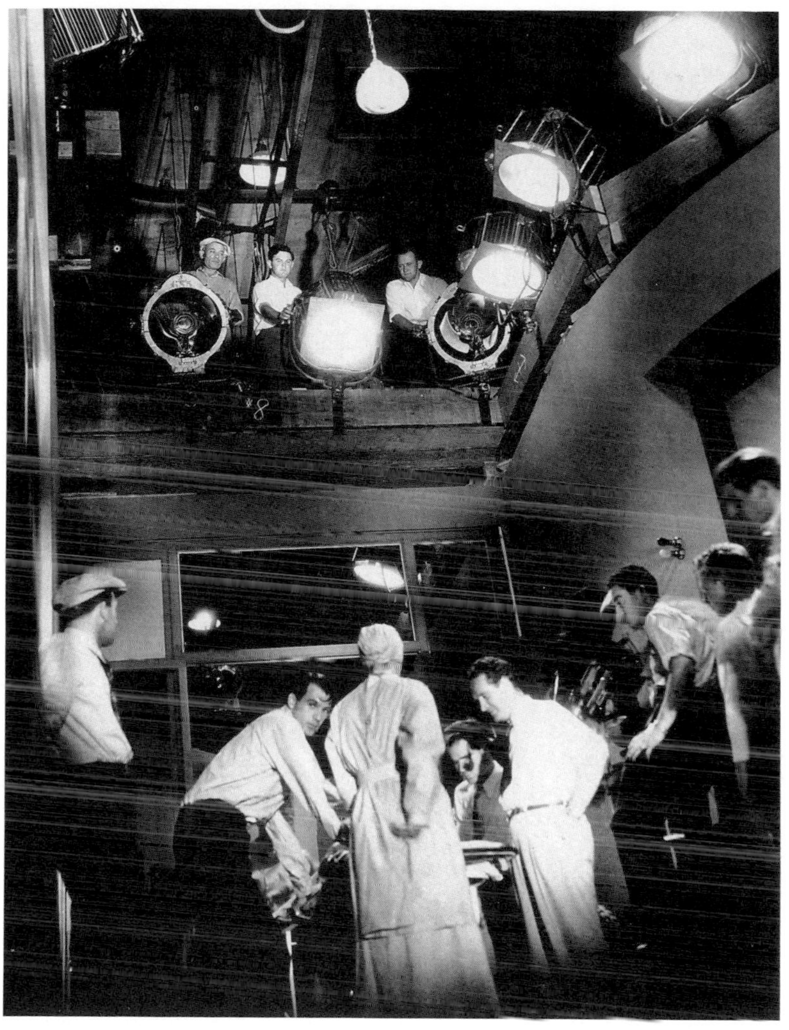

Preparing a scene for the epic production of *A Farewell to Arms*. Gary Cooper left of table, director Frank Borzage standing right of table, Arthur Jacobson second from right. 1933.

Courtesy of the Academy of Motion Picture Arts and Sciences

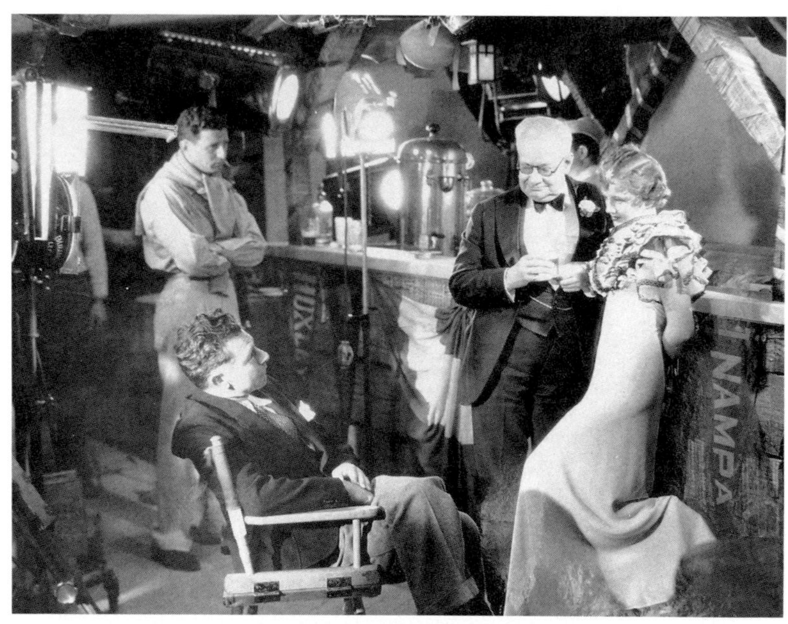

On the set of *Shoot the Works*. Left to right, Arthur Jacobson, director Wesley Ruggles, unidentified actor, Arline Judge. 1934.

Jacobson's directorial effort for Paramount was *Home on the Range*. Left to right, William Mellor (cameraman), Randolph Scott, Jacobson, Evelyn Brent, Sid Street (unit manager), Fritz Collins. Standing behind Sid Street is Jack Dennis (cutter). September 1934.

True Confession. Left to right, Fred MacMurray, Carole Lombard, Tom Dugan, Una Merkel, Paul Weatherwax (cutter), Wesley Ruggles, Arthur Jacobson, script girl, Romayne Goldsmith, Ted Tetzlaff, Dan Fapp. 1937.

True Confession. Left to right, Wesley Ruggles, Claude Binyon (writer), Paul Weatherwax, Carole Lombard, John Barrymore. 1937.

Making the "Switzerland" sequences at Sun Valley, California, for *I Met Him in Paris*. 1937.

At the Pomona fairgrounds for the race track sequence of *Sing You Sinners*. Seated, script girl, Wesley Ruggles. Standing, Arthur Jacobson (with cigarotte), Bing Crosby. On horse, Donald O'Connor. 1938.

Wesley Ruggles, Donald O'Connor, and Ellen Drew during the production of *Sing You Sinners*, 1938. Arthur Jacobson became Head of Talent at Paramount in 1939 after discovering new talents O'Connor and Drew.

Rehearsal for CBS radio version of *Sing You Sinners*. Left to right, Wesley Ruggles, Donald O'Connor, Fred MacMurray, Arthur Jacobson. 1938.

On location for *I Wanted Wings*. Standing on ladder, director Mitchell Leisen; standing behind camera, Leo Tover (cameraman); seated under camera, Arthur Jacobson; facing front, Ray Milland; leaning on cockpit, William Holden. 1941.

Courtesy of the Academy of Motion Picture Arts and Sciences

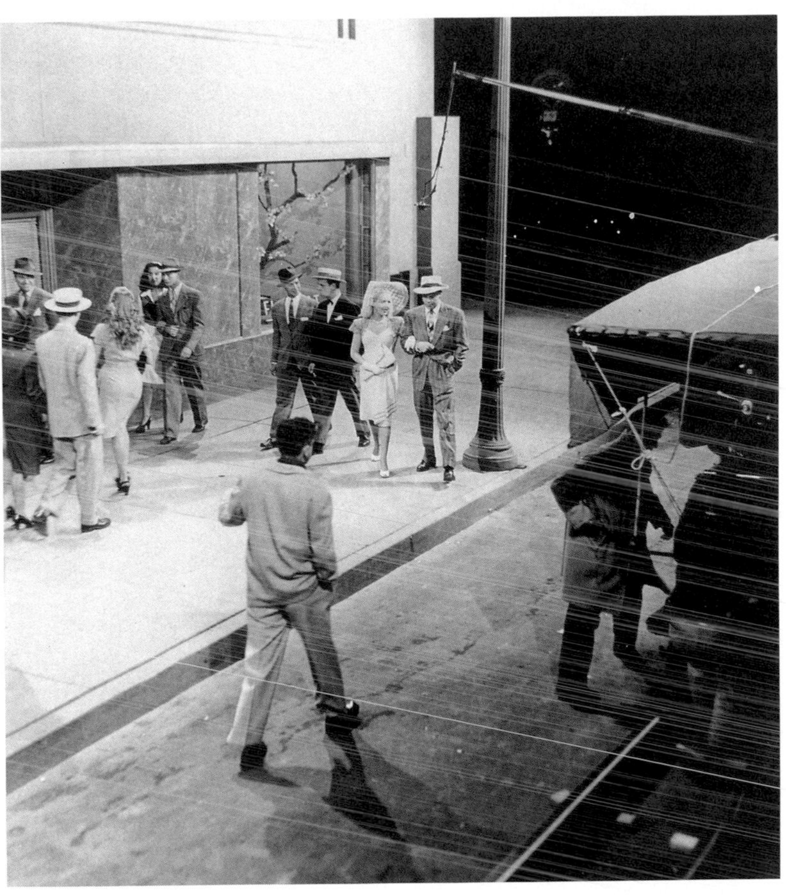

Jacobson directing background action for the musical *Diamond Horseshoe*. Left of lamppost, Betty Grable and Dick Haymes. 1945.
Courtesy of the Academy of Motion Picture Arts and Sciences

On the backstage set of *The Dolly Sisters*. Left to right, Howard Koch (assistant), Arthur Jacobson, director Irving Cummings, Betty Grable. Miss Grable and Arthur became friends and she inscribed a photo thanking him for the great doughnuts he brought her on the set. 1945.
Courtesy of the Academy of Motion Picture Arts and Sciences

Centennial Summer, a Fox costume musical. Director Otto Preminger with hand on camera, Arthur Jacobson standing far right. 1946.

Arthur Jacobson presenting director George Seaton with the *Photoplay* Blue Ribbon Picture of the Month Award for *Miracle on 34th Street*. 1947.

The Utah location set for *Thunder in the Valley*. Left to right, Duke Gooy (second unit manager), Peggy Ann Garner's mother, Arthur Jacobson, Peggy Ann Garner, Louis King, Mrs. King, Reginald Owen, studio location nurse, script clerk, technical director, Lon McCallister, Charles Irwin. 1947.

A happy moment in Hawaii during the near-catastrophic South Seas adventure with director Julien Duvivier. Left to right, unidentified host, Mrs. Duvivier, Gloria Jacobson, Duvivier, unidentified hostess, Arthur Jacobson. 1948.

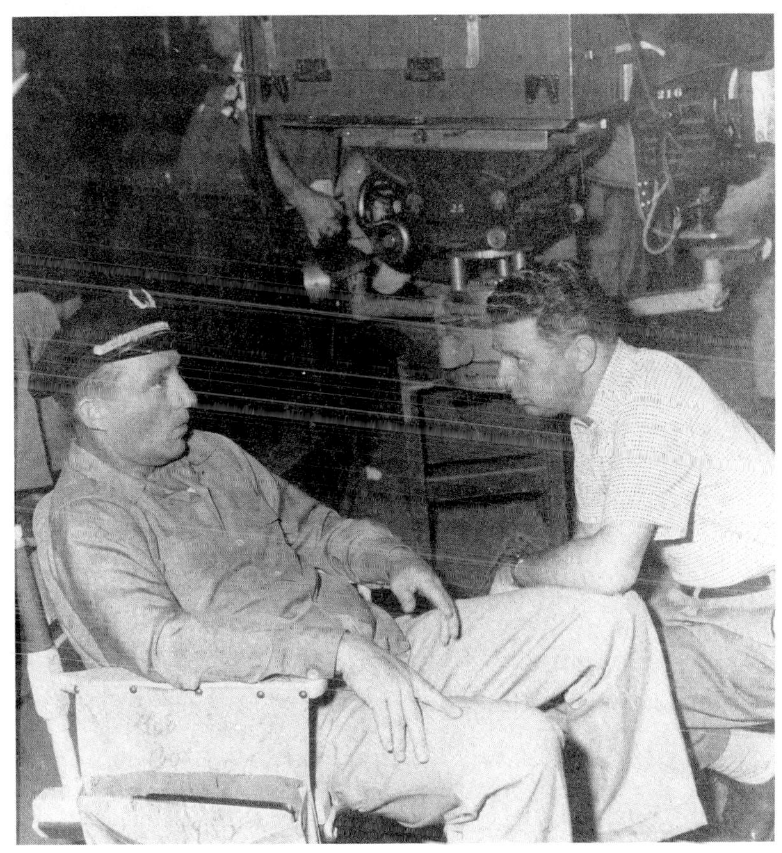

Conferring with friend Bing Crosby on the set of *Little Boy Lost*. 1952.

Richard Harris entertains Arthur Jacobson on the set of *Camelot*. 1967.

wisps. You might be having lunch with someone who told you about a performer in Florida, and by six o'clock you'd be on a plane for Florida to see the person.

In 1940, I went to New York to make some tests and rented space at the Long Island Studios, which were no longer Paramount. I made a test of a girl, but when I brought the test out here, the studio wouldn't buy her, even though I tried to convince them that they should. They said her starting salary was too high. At the end of the option, which is thirty days, I was rather angry that the studio did not take her, so I released the test to other studios, and within forty-eight hours she was at Warner Brothers. Her name was Brenda Marshall, and she eventually married Bill Holden. I had nothing to do with their getting together.

One Monday morning I went over to Oblath's for a cup of coffee and I read in *The Hollywood Reporter* that I had been demoted. That made me mad. They told me on the phone to come back to the studio for a meeting, which I did, and I found out that Henry Ginsburg was responsible. I didn't even know who he was. I went into his office and did another stupid thing, like the thing that cost me a directorship.

I said, "Why are you doing this?"

He said, "I don't have to explain to you why I'm changing. You're going back into production."

I said, "No I'm not, unless I choose to. Incidentally, what is your function around here?"

He got up and reached across his desk and did what the other guy had done. He shook his finger in my nose and I hit him on the wrist, and got out of the office.

I had this great track record but even with my record, here was a man who stepped right in, put me back in production, and brought in his friend, Bill Meiklejohn, who was also my friend, to take my job without telling me about it.

That's why I had a particular hatred for Henry Ginsburg. I didn't care about the talent job, but I was embarrassed, angry, and hurt.

ATKINS: Is that when you went to *I Wanted Wings*?

JACOBSON: Yes. We started *I Wanted Wings* in the summertime, with great heat. The director was a man who had been Arthur Hornblow's associate, Ted Reid. He had been president of the Academy at one time. He was a brilliant man, and this was his opportunity to make a big, big picture. We went down to Texas and Ted bent the elbow a little bit. We found out after the first day that Ted should not drink at night because the heat of the day was too much for him. We had towels dipped in ice water to wrap around him while he was sweating it out, and we had a big umbrella over him.

On the third day of shooting Ted got a telegram from Arthur Hornblow. There was a disagreement about how a scene should be shot. In the telegram, Hornblow mentioned some scenes that had been in another of his pictures that Mitchell Leisen had directed. Hornblow had made quite a few pictures with Leisen, who was a very artistic director.

Ted said, "If he wants Mitchell Leisen, let him get Mitchell Leisen."

At about two o'clock in the morning, there was a knock on the door, and it was Reid. He showed me a letter he had written to Hornblow, saying the same sort of things about "Why don't you get Leisen."

I told him not to mail the letter, but the Scotch was talking, and he dropped it in the mail chute. The following day there was a call to take Ted Reid to the airport and have him fly back to Hollywood for a meeting at the studio.

We all said, "What an opportunity this guy is kicking in the butt."

We got a telephone call, "Meet the plane tomorrow morning." We did, and out stepped Mitchell Leisen. He took over. Mitch was a brilliant man.

Arthur Hornblow, in casting *I Wanted Wings*, came up with Veronica Lake. I must say one thing for him: he had an instinct. We made some wardrobe and hair tests, and in one of the tests, in turning around, her hair fell over one eye. We went right on with the test. He took one look at it and said, "I want her hair that way. I have a feeling it can create a fad."

It did. You had gals all over the world with their hair hanging over one eye.

With the cooperation of the Air Force, we went to Randolph Field and Kelly Field in Texas, came back and went to March Field, and then to Hamilton Field.

ATKINS: Why did you have to go to so many different airfields? Couldn't all the location shooting have been done at one place?

JACOBSON: No, the story called for that. One field was for basic training, another for advanced, one for B-17s, and so on.

Ray Milland had been a pilot, in England, I think. He wanted to fly one of the planes for a minute, and the pilot in charge let him do it. The plane wavered a little bit, and we didn't like it. It was against all rules. He shouldn't have been allowed to do it.

ATKINS: This must have been made just before the war started.

JACOBSON: It was made in 1940, but released in 1941.

ATKINS: Anything else about *I Wanted Wings*?

JACOBSON: Yes. We had a wonderful actor named Richard Lane. I said to the powers that be, "Don't take any of the actors up in a plane without checking with me first." One day, I called for Dick Lane, and we couldn't find him. An instructor stepped up to me and said, "Mr. Lane is having a joy-ride with one of the boys." They contacted the tower and got him down.

When Dick got out of the plane in full uniform, I said, "Dick, never do that again. I've covered up for you for the scene, but I want to teach you a lesson." I asked for a penknife, and I slit open his parachute. All the sawdust fell out on the floor. It was a fake parachute. He turned yellow, green, white. So that was a cure for that.

Constance Moore was in the picture. She and Veronica didn't get along too well.

Arthur Hornblow had sent a woman down to Texas to be Veronica Lake's chaperon, because we knew she bent the elbow. She had a thing with Hornblow. As a matter of fact it came out later because it broke up his home, when he divorced Myrna Loy.

We invited the major-domo's wife to visit the set, which was on the flying line. She was very thrilled, and was sitting in a director's chair. Now all through this, even when we weren't working, there were boys walking amongst the airplanes out to their assignments. These were propeller planes, so you'd better watch where you were going.

Mrs. Major-Domo, crooked her finger, called me over, and said, "You'd better stop that. That isn't done around here. We're going to have an accident."

I turned and looked, and there, with a publicity man — who was at fault — was Veronica Lake, in a skin-tight white bathing suit with her arms outstretched and her chest stuck out, standing up on the wing of a plane, having still pictures made. All these boys who were walking towards their planes were looking back over their shoulders at the luscious thing. We stopped that in a hurry.

The cast and crew were invited to the cadet hop which was just before graduation. It was at the Gunther Roof, a hotel downtown. I decided to keep my eye on Veronica Lake, because she could embarrass the pants off of you. After a while she excused herself to go to the ladies' room, which was up a flight of stairs, with a big banister. As she started down the stairs, she had her evening gown hiked up and she was ready to slide down the banister. I was there in nothing flat, and escorted her down the stairs and out the door, walked her back to the hotel, and practically locked her in her room. Where was her chaperon? She was asleep.

ATKINS: Were you involved in planning the flying sequences in *I Wanted Wings*?

JACOBSON: No. We told them what we wanted. But an interesting thing happened at the graduation of the cadets. It took place outdoors and we duplicated it. They lined up all the planes, ninety-eight of them, all flying in echelon, in groups of four. As they came across, over the graduating class, they dipped, all of them. That's not too difficult because it's all done mathematically. But in the middle of the dip one of them wavered. Major Davis, a man who was about five-foot-six, with a little moustache, was absolutely ashen, because if that boy didn't get hold of that thing in the next split second there could be an awful tragedy. Fortunately the kid did it. It's still on film.

ATKINS: Were there any problems with any of the flying sequences?

JACOBSON: No, none at all. But before the picture was over we had to go to the Mission Inn to shoot some scenes. Veronica Lake was supposed to be in the scenes, and one Monday morning, we were ready to shoot, but there was no Veronica Lake. We had to switch and do this and that. We found out that Miss Lake had disappeared and gotten married over the weekend. She didn't tell anybody about it, and to hell with her call Monday morning. She married this guy and was on her honeymoon.

To backtrack a minute about *I Wanted Wings* — when we went down there with Ted Reid, Hedda Hopper was going to play the mother of one of the flyers. After the change in director was made, they rewrote the script. Here she sat on location, ready to work, and we had to tell her that she had been written out of the script. They sent her home. They paid her, but she was quite angry about it.

ATKINS: Her name is listed in the cast.

JACOBSON: Well, she's not in the picture. But to get back to Veronica Lake. We finally finished the location shots, and went back to the studio to finish all of the interiors. Monday morning there was to be a scene with three hundred cadets. I got there about 6:30 that morning — I always got to the studio at least two hours ahead of call time — checked everything, and had my assistant check the makeup department. Everybody was there except Veronica.

We called her home, but there was no answer. We sent a studio car to her house and found that she hadn't been home all night, and now it was almost shooting time. I told Mitchell Leisen, and he really got teed off. We had to move over to another set, after we'd lost all that work with the three hundred extras.

I tried to figure out where she might be. She had married an MGM art director, John DeCuir. I called the

MGM production office, and asked what picture he was on. They told me and I said, "Is he there?"

They said, "No, he's on location in Phoenix."

Ah hah! They told me the name of the hotel in Phoenix where the company was staying. I called there and asked to talk to Mr. DeCuir.

They said, "He's out on location."

I said, "Let me talk to Mrs. DeCuir."

They said, "She's with him."

I told them to leave a note for her to call me as soon as she came in. Her husband called me and I said, "You'd better tell her to get her ass back here if she wants to stay in this business, because I've got a fiery-tempered director who is just ready to kill her."

He put her in an automobile and started her for the airport. There was an automobile accident and she got a broken ankle. They put her on a train, and she finally arrived at the studio two or three days later.

At that point there was a scene in the tail of a B-17, which was cone-shaped and small. She came on the set with crutches. She started to say something to Mitchell and he let her have it. He said to me, "Get her in position, in the tail."

We tried to help her in, but the pain was terrible. Again he said, "Get her in the plane."

He insisted that she had to try to do the scene without crying. We finally got it done, and she became a star.

When I went on location with *I Wanted Wings,* I was gone for about six months. I never went near the studio, and I was thankful for that because I was embarrassed. When I did get back to the studio I was so busy that I almost forgot about it. Every once in a while I'd pass Henry Ginsburg on the lot.

When the picture was almost finished, Keith Glennon, who was a telephone company executive, had become production manager. He called me into his office and said, "Artie, you're getting yourself in trouble. Every time Henry Ginsburg sees you on the lot he salutes you and you cut him dead."

I said, "Oh, I didn't know he was that sensitive. How can I cut anybody dead who doesn't exist?"

He said, "Unless you change your attitude, it's your job."

I said, "Don't lecture me. Just fire me. I will not resign. Just fire me, and I'm going to have quite a few things to say to the Guild. I'll see to it that what Henry Ginsburg did to me will be known."

I never did. I wasn't that kind of a guy.

Christmas came and I was out. I bid farewell and drove off into the sunset from Paramount Studios, saying, "I will never set foot in a studio again if Henry Ginsburg is connected with it," and I never did.

About two weeks later the comptroller, a man named A. C. Martin, called me and said, "Will you come to the studio? I have something for you."

I said, "No. I made a vow never to come to the studio."

He said, "I think it's money."

I said, "I'll be right over. But I'm coming in the back way."

There was a check for five thousand dollars. Martin said he didn't know who had authorized it. So, as they say, I took the money and ran. I couldn't find out who had authorized it. I started looking for a job.

Ten years later, when I was at Fox, with George Seaton and Bill Perlberg, I found out about the check I had received. After I had been at Fox a long time, been given many promises and directed second units in many places, Mr. George Seaton came to me and said, "We are severing our connections with Fox. We're going to become Perlberg-Seaton Productions, an independent, but at a major studio. I'd like you to join us as our associate. We'll get another assistant director. We'll pay you a little more money, and maybe over a period of time you'll get a picture to direct. I'll see to that."

I didn't tell Ray Clune, my boss, yet but accepted the offer anyway. Clune found out about it, called me in and asked if it was true. I said, "Yes."

"Why?"

I told him. "I've been here so many years, and as far as promises are concerned, I've never even met Zanuck. Nobody even thinks I'm important enough to be introduced to him. But I've made up my mind."

He got a little angry with Bill Perlberg. I didn't realize it but there always had been bad blood between him and Bill Perlberg. Not to get back at me, because Ray and I were good friends, but to get back at Perlberg he reported this incident to Zanuck.

Zanuck was a little annoyed because George and Bill were leaving him. He sent a letter to Ray and said, "This man Jacobson, his heart is no longer with us. Immediately on completion of his present assignment, relieve him of his duties at Twentieth Century-Fox."

I went to George and said, "I'm in a spot. Between now and the time you do something, I may not get paid."

He said, "Don't worry about it. No matter where we go, it will be retroactive, even if I have to pay it out of my own pocket. You're not going to lose any money on it."

Two days later he came to me and said, "We just signed with Paramount."

I said I couldn't go back to Paramount, and told him the whole story about my leaving there.

He said, "You hate Ginsburg, don't you? How do you get along with Freeman?"

I said, "Fine. I think he had something to do with the five thousand dollars I got."

Two days later George called me in and said, "You're going to Paramount with us. They're firing Ginsburg, now. He was there for ten years. I want you to come to the studio tomorrow and have lunch with us."

I said, "Will he be there?"

"No. I think they've already moved everything out of his office."

Some time later, we were going to a preview in San Diego, and after some mixup, I landed in the back seat of a studio car with Y. Frank Freeman. We had a two-hour trip, and finally I said, "Mr. Freeman, for ten years I have had something nagging at me. When I left Paramount, I got some money. Did you do it?"

He said, "Yes, I did. We'll make up for what happened. You're not the only one. We made a mistake."

The thing that caused Ginsburg's dismissal was that he tried to take over Freeman's job and be the head of the studio. But Freeman was too powerful.

ATKINS: I understand that Ginsburg was not too well-liked by the backlot people.

JACOBSON: He was despised by everybody. He was a hatchet man.

When I left Paramount, I called David O. Selznick for an appointment, and the secretary said to come over the next evening. Selznick always did things at night. David was the only man I ever wrote a fan letter to. It was after I saw *Intermezzo*.

I knew him well, because he had been a young producer at Paramount and I'd done many pictures with him.

I went to the studio in Culver City, where his office was as big as Grand Central Station, and you sank up to your ankles in carpeting. He got up from behind his desk, came around and shook hands with me. After I sat down, the first thing he said was, "I hear you ran afoul of Henry Ginsburg."

"How did you know?"

"It's my business to know a lot of things. When you asked to come and see me, I wanted to find out why you weren't at Paramount anymore, and I learned that you'd refused to knuckle down to Ginsburg. Tell me about it."

I had a friendly ear, so I talked over an hour, and everything I had in me spilled out. He never once interrupted me. Then he said, "Go home. God bless you. You'll hear from me."

Selznick had fired Henry Ginsburg from his studio for doing a few unethical things.

Three days later I got a call from Ray Clune, who was Selznick's production manager. He said that Mr. Selznick had a little project he'd like me to do. He was between productions, he had four young men he wanted tested, and he wanted me to direct the tests. Ray asked me how I would like to go about it.

I said, "I'd like to meet the four men and read the material David wants to use. Then we'll decide which man should do what, and we'll talk about production."

The next day I met the men. One of them was Cornel Wilde, who was unknown. I don't remember who the others were. I took the material home, and my heart sank. For the life of me, I couldn't fit any of it to the four actors. All the time I had been in the talent department, I had taken luscious scenes out of scripts and radio programs. Somehow I convinced Ray, and Selznick in turn, to let me use my material.

I met the men again, and distributed the scenes they were to do. Cornel Wilde balked and said, "I want to do a Shakespearean scene."

I said, "If you do, you've got the wrong man. I don't know beans about Shakespeare. I can hurt you and myself by making a bad test." He dropped the idea.

The next morning we shot. We used the Samuel Goldwyn Studio. I suggested a trick — we had three different sets, and it was going to be an expensive day. I said, "I can do it in one day if you let me start at seven o'clock in the morning. I'll be through by two the next morning. Give me three telescoped sets — a large set, a smaller set inside of it, and a smaller set inside of that, like Chinese boxes. I'll shoot the smallest set first. I'll be through with it by lunch, and during the break they can yank it out. By dinnertime we'll be through with the second set and we'll yank it out."

We shot the stuff, and I called Ray the next morning. I said, "When can I see the rushes?"

"Oh," he said, "the film is now David's. Nobody looks at rushes, only David."

I said, "What do you mean? How could he possibly know how to cut it? I'm the only one who knows how to cut it, because I shot it."

I asked to talk to David, and told Ray that I insisted that I have the first cut. He called me back and said, "I don't know what influence you have over this man, but you've got it."

I went over to the cutting room. I was there for two or three nights, and I was very satisfied with it. Now mind you, I hadn't seen David all this time, only a man named Danny O'Shea.

I went home, and three days later I got a check in the mail for three times the basis of a test director, with a wonderful, wonderful note that said, "David wants to see you."

I went over and he said, "I like what you did. You've got great potential. I'll get a hold of Danny O'Shea and we'll draw up a three-way contract. You can be an assistant director or production manager for me and eventually a director. You'll gradually work into it."

I said, "I don't care what you want me to do. I'll do it."

He also said, "We'll see to it that the money is right. You'll get over scale."

He didn't make another picture for many years. He eventually made *A Farewell to Arms,* which was a bust. Then David died. There went my great opportunity — the greatest opportunity I ever had in my life.

Working with Henry Hathaway

ATKINS: Somewhere in this period after you left Paramount you worked with Henry Hathaway.

JACOBSON: Yes. It was in 1941 on a picture called *Sundown*. Henry was a very dear personal friend, and I went to him personally. He was going to do this picture for Walter Wanger. It was an independent production for United Artists. Walter was being financed by the bank, so consequently they had a man from the bank, who was going to oversee the expenditures, right there in the studio. The producer under Wanger was Jack Moss.

It was an overscale job and a long one. We were going to go all over the place and look for locations. I went through Henry, Walter Wanger, and Jack Moss. All of a sudden Walter said to me, "Wait a minute. Your salary has to be okayed by Mr. Lehr, the representative of the bank. Just go down there and schmooze him."

My salary was so-and-so. I was welcomed by Mr. Lehr the minute I walked in. He was a very nice man who had one job to do: get everything as cheaply as you can. He said, "You know, there's only one thing. We're not going to start this picture for quite a while, and you're going to go on this pleasure trip with Mr. Hathaway for four to six weeks."

I said, "I beg your pardon? Have you ever looked for locations Mr. Lehr, especially with Mr. Hathaway? It's not a pleasure trip — it's work. You work twenty-four hours a day, and you go to very strange places."

He said, "Nevertheless, I wondered if you would work for those few weeks while you're looking for locations, at scale," which was about fifty dollars a week less than I was going to get.

I said to myself, "Why you cheap — ," but I smiled, using my hypocritical face, and said out loud, "If the company is that tight on money — I want the job. If that's the way it'll be, I'll do it."

He said, "You don't have to talk it over with Mr. Hathaway."

I said, "Fine. It's none of Mr. Hathaway's concern." He didn't want me to talk to Henry, because Henry would scream bloody murder.

I went out of his office, went down the hall to the men's room, and then went right back to his office and said, "Oh, Mr. Lehr, there's something I forgot. You were so kind to me, and in my enthusiasm about the job — I have to check this out with my guild. I have to notify the Guild that I'm accepting the position and what the salary is, and all the conditions. I don't know how to explain to them that my salary is going to be scale for four to six weeks and then it's going to go higher. You help me explain this to them, because it's rather unusual. I don't think they've ever heard of such a thing."

He said, "Oh, you have to check this out with the Directors Guild?"

"Yes, but they'll be in touch with you. I wouldn't worry about it."

He said, "Just a second. Just forget the whole thing. Don't contact the Guild about the salary. Just tell them what you have to tell them, and the salary will be the regular full salary right from the beginning."

I said, "Thank you, Mr. Lehr. That will save an awful lot of trouble." We shook hands and I walked out. I went up and told Wanger about it and he laughed. I never did tell Henry, though, because if I had, he would have gotten on this guy's tail and his life would have been miserable.

Henry and I had an understanding — if Henry wanted to swear, he could, but he would never swear at me in front of the company. Otherwise I would walk out on him — much as I wanted the job.

ATKINS: You did go all over looking for locations.

JACOBSON: Oh! Just Henry and I, in his car. We went all over the Southwest and Northwest, for four to six weeks, and we finally wound up in the southwestern tip of New Mexico, which is where the caves are. We went from Carlsbad, clear up to the northwestern tip, up through Santa Fe and Albuquerque.

ATKINS: Where was the action supposed to be taking place?

JACOBSON: Africa. We finally decided on an Indian village called Acoma, Sky City, on the top of a plateau. There was nothing there. We had two hundred sixteen people, and Hathaway said, "Let them pitch a camp." It was windy and blizzardy. There wasn't snow, but the wind got into your nostrils and under your eyelids. It was miserable, believe me.

Gene Tierney, George Sanders and Reginald Gardiner were in the picture. We had a wonderful unit manager. I haven't been saying nice things about unit managers, but this one was a wonderful guy named Danny Keefe. Charles Lang was the cameraman.

We made arrangements to rent a herd of goats from one Indian, who had a little corral built against the rocks, and we were going to use the goats all through the picture. On the first payday we heard that he was telling everyone that we had cheated him. Through an interpreter we found out what was wrong. We were to pay him a dollar a day, but he said we owed him 14 dollars, not the seven we'd paid him. You see, to an Indian a day is from sunup to sundown, and we'd also had the goats from sundown to sunup, so that was the same as seven extra days. So we paid him the other seven dollars, and that was settled.

There was a wild man, whom I shared a tent with in the camp, Ernest Westmore, of the great Westmores. He was the make-up man. Henry insisted, from research, that the native women be bald, because the women in Africa were bald. We needed at least twelve bald-headed Negro women. We decided to try to get twelve women from Albuquerque. We promised them fifty dollars, a wig until their hair grew back, and we threw in a hat.

Ernie Westmore said, "Don't ask the women. Ask their husbands." Sure enough, we went there and talked to the guys. They signed a piece of paper, and they were all going to get fifty bucks. We took the women up to the make-up department, and it didn't take long until we had bald women. Henry wanted to know how we'd gotten them to do it, but we wouldn't tell him.

We had made it a business to try to get fifty couples from Albuquerque, who lived at the camp to be extras in the picture. It made it easier for living.

The opening scene of the picture shows a caravan of camels, zebras, and all sort of animals, being led by Gene Tierney. We wanted to panic all these animals, so we had pots, pans, and anything that would make noise attached to them. Paul Mantz was our man with the airplanes. We had a radio, and on a signal he was to buzz the caravan and make a lot of noise. Paul came in, b-r-r-r-m-m. Not a thing happened.

Hathaway jumped up and down, screaming bloody murder. "Artie, do something about it!"

I went down into the caravan, put a burnoose on, blackened my face and I was part of the group. I was in the middle of the pack, next to a camel and its baby, and I had a long stick with a nail on the end of it. This time when the plane went over them I let the camel have it. I goosed it. Well, all hell broke loose, but the little baby camel turned around and kicked me and knocked me flat on my face. Hathaway screamed with laughter at that. It was all on film and the panic looked fine.

When we got back to Samuel Goldwyn Studios, we had caves, greenery, and a lake. In the scene, the government agents are chasing the heavy at night and firing at him. It's completely dark but you can see the tracer bullets. The only way you can see tracer bullets is to use real live ammunition — you can't fake it. There was supposed to be just one pin-spot on the man.

I explained to Henry that the bullets were liable to ricochet, but that if the sharpshooters who were working were on target and everyone stayed exactly in their places and nobody moved, it would work. Henry said I could handle the whole thing, and I explained through the loudspeaker, "When I say, lights out, every light on this stage will be out. From that point on, nobody move! Don't even breathe!"

We tried everything, and the cameras were ready. I was standing right by the water, and as the lights went out and I was saying, "Nobody move," I backed up two steps and went right in the drink, over my head. Fortunately they heard the splash. I came up and I yelled, "Lights!"

I was the sorriest looking thing. I thought Henry was going to bust a gut laughing. I got some dry clothes out of wardrobe, and I looked even worse. But we got the scene. That's the way it goes.

ATKINS: Two cameramen are listed for *Sundown,* Charles Lang and Ray Binger.

JACOBSON: Ray Binger was the process cameraman, and he was to go out and shoot some beautiful cloud stuff. In New Mexico the clouds come and go. One morning Ray came to me and said, "The clouds are beautiful. I'll go shoot them."

By the time he got packed up, the clouds had disappeared. An hour later he came back to me and said, "Here they are again."

Henry got a little excited and said, "Oh, for Christ's sake, if you're going to shoot it, shoot it."

I said, "Henry, keep your pants on. We just want you to know you're not going to have Ray here this morning."

It happened a second and third time, and Hathaway started to scream, "There we go with that goddamn thing again. Send the guy for the goddamn cloud stuff right now, and if he comes back without it, I'm telling you right now it's your ass."

I said, "Ray, go get the stuff."

As I mentioned, I had made arrangements with Henry that he was never to shout or use profanity at me in front of the company or do anything that would jeopardize my control of the company. I went to my assistant and said, "Stand by Hathaway and work with him." Everything was ready and Henry said, "Artie!"

A voice from fifty yards away said, "Yes?" Here I was up on a rock in the sun, stripped to the waist sunning myself. He said, "Let's go."

I said, "I'm not your assistant any more. I'm going back to Hollywood. You've forgotten the agreement we made." I walked down, and we continued talking. I reminded him of what he'd said to me. I went to my tent and started packing. He called off the day's shooting and came in there.

I said, "I'll call Wanger and get you another assistant. I've taken enough from you in trying to keep this company together, because you drive everybody nuts the way you insult them and scream and holler. You've got an art director that's on the verge of suicide, Alexander Golitzen." He was. He used to cry.

Hathaway kept saying he hadn't sworn or said anything insulting to me. I called in Charlie Lang and said, "Charlie, I'm putting you on the spot, but you were right there when this happened. Right?"

"Right."

Wanger got on the phone and asked me not to leave.

"I won't leave you in the lurch, but send somebody down immediately."

He never did, and I never quit. At the end of the picture, Henry sent me a beautiful portable barbecue. I sent it back to him. He sent it back to me. Then Charlie Lang's wife borrowed it. This was in 1940. She's had it ever since.

Henry was not good to work with, but he was a good friend. When we wanted to build our house, Henry called me and said, "When are you going to build your house?"

I said, "Not for another year. I can't afford it. Prices have gone so sky-high, and unless I can afford it I'm not going to build it."

He said, "A year from now prices will be even higher. How much do you need?"

I told him: twenty-five hundred dollars, which was a lot of money for me. An hour later a kid came in my office and handed me an envelope. In it was a check for twenty-five hundred dollars and a note, "Build your house."

I took it home to Gloria and said, "What about it?"

She called him on the phone and said, "I'll accept the loan on one condition — I pay it back in a year with bank interest."

He said, "Do whatever you goddamn please, but build your house."

We paid it back in six months. He sent the second check for bank interest back, all torn up.

The morning we turned a shovel to build the house, it was eight o'clock in the morning and Henry was right there. My wife walked up to him and said, "Henry darling, we love you, you helped build the house with the money, but from this point on, keep your nose out of it. Get out of here! I don't want you around when they're building this house. When it's built you and Skip will be welcome to it, but don't tell us how to build it."

To the end of his life, Henry and I were great friends. But we could not get along on a set.

ATKINS: Could anyone get along with him? How about the actors?

JACOBSON: Henry had a pet peeve against one actor. I'll never know why. His name was Carl Esmond. He gave him a very bad time, but Carl stuck it through.

One of the leads in the cast was Joseph Calleia. One day at lunchtime he called me into his dressing room. He was in tears — he had had too much. He was so confused and upset that he couldn't work. He asked me to go to Mr. Wanger and find out how much it would cost to be replaced. He wanted to pay him every nickel, rather than go back on the set, because he could not work with Mr. Hathaway.

By the same token, we had George Sanders. Henry couldn't flap him for one second. He may have been going crazy inside, but the more Henry yelled, the quieter George Sanders got. He always got his way.

I went to Henry with definite remarks. I never said, "Maybe we'll do so-and-so." I would say, "At 10:15 we're going to do so-and-so." He liked that kind of stuff and we always made it stick.

One particular time Gene Tierney had a costume and hair change. I said, "Right after the next take is printed, we'll send Gene in for that change. It will take forty-six minutes." That got a grin out of Henry.

He said, "Cut,"

I said, "All right, everybody, change, forty-six minutes." About fifteen minutes went by, and Henry and Charlie were ready for the next set-up. Henry used to waddle like an elephant. He'd rock from side to side, chew on his cigar, and pull at his hair. After about eighteen minutes he said, "Where is she?"

I said, "Eighteen from forty-six; that's how much longer it's going to take." We waited another few minutes.

"Artie, for Christ's sakes, will you get the gal out here?"

I said, "I told you, there's at least another fifteen minutes to go, but I'll get her if you want her the way she is."

He said, "Fine."

I went over and knocked on her door. I said, "Gene, the man wants you."

She opened the door and came out in a black bra and black pants — very nice to look at — and got right in front of the camera and said, "Mr. Hathaway, you have me. Shall we rehearse and shoot?"

He said, "Get your costume on!"

She said, "I can't. You won't let me. I can't do my hair. Leave me alone! I love you."

She walked out and went back to her dressing room. Henry turned around to me and said, "Why do you put me in such a spot?"

I said, "You put yourself in such a spot. Henry, you're nuts!" That's the way we used to get along.

The last time I saw him was at George Seaton's funeral. All I said to him was, "Henry, how about one night you and Skip fix spaghetti the way you used to, in the 1920s?"

He said, "My God, what a memory. But you don't eat spaghetti. You're getting a little fat." I never saw him again.

A Move to Fox

ATKINS: How did you happen to start working at Twentieth Century-Fox Studios?

JACOBSON: That's a long story. I was between pictures, and something came along through the Screen Directors Guild. Certain people, like Mark Sandrich and me, became connected with a patriotic venture for the war called *The Hollywood Victory Caravan.*

Mark Sandrich produced and directed., and the executive in charge was Charles Feldman. Allan Scott was the head writer, and there were several other big writers. All the music writers were in on it, including Johnny Mercer and Irving Berlin, and Al Newman conducted the orchestra. We took ten men with us and augmented them in each city. We usually had sixty men in the orchestra pit. Al Fisher was in charge of that.

I was asked to go along as Mark's assistant, and I was pleased to accept. It was a patriotic thing to do. We rehearsed at the Paramount rehearsal hall, for four weeks, and went to Washington in a ten-car train, with two diners. The cars were made up of drawing rooms and compartments only. There was one club car, in which Al rehearsed his music and Mark rehearsed his acts.

We had Laurel and Hardy, Bob Hope, Bing Crosby and Cary Grant as the M. C.'s. In the cast were Bert Lahr, Olivia de Havilland, Marlene Dietrich, Groucho Marx, Joan Blondell, Jimmy Cagney, Pat O'Brien and others.

Later, Fred Astaire, Hedy Lamarr, Joan Crawford, Judy Garland, Mickey Rooney, and many others went out.

Mrs. Roosevelt attended the Washington, D. C. performance, though FDR could not be there.

No outsiders were allowed on that train. We had our own photographer and each star was allowed to destroy any of their pictures if they didn't want them published.

ATKINS: Did any husbands or wives go along?

JACOBSON: No. They all stayed home. We had Desi Arnaz, but Lucille didn't go along. We had six of the most beautiful girls in town as chorus girls. Charlotte Greenwood was the matriarch of the whole bunch — a wonderful person. Because she was an old trouper, she showed them how to string a piece of clothesline across the car, wash their stuff, and hang it out during the night.

ATKINS: Did they do the same show in every city?

JACOBSON: Yes. Every act went on in each town. Microphones had to be used for everything because the places were so huge. There was no regular intermission. When the intermission time came, they auctioned off things, like autographed programs, to make money for the Fund. Claudette Colbert was with us, and in one city a man up in the balcony said he would give a thousand dollars if Claudette would kiss him. She turned to me and said, "Take me up there."

In her evening gown, she hiked up to the balcony, and said to him, "Give me the check." He handed her a check, she kissed him, and there was great applause.

We'd arrive at each town at noon, and go on at night. We'd have a parade from the railroad station to the hotel where we were staying, with the local Boy Scouts, Girl Scouts, and Marines. They carried a huge flag, and people would throw money into the flag. We would stop enroute, and the sailors would run into nearby markets to get boxes and, with their white hats, they'd scoop the money out of the flag and throw it into the boxes.

When we got to the hotel in the first town, Groucho Marx was in tears. The crowds on the sidewalk had cheered all the stars. Groucho didn't even get a hand, and he was grumpy. I went to him and said, "What's the matter?"

He said, "They don't even know me. They hate me."

Somebody, I don't remember who, came up and said, "Of course, they didn't know you. You don't have your moustache on."

From then on, we put the names of the stars on the windshields.

When we got to the town at noon, half the tickets were sold. After the parade, every ticket was sold, standing room only.

When the tour was all over, quite a few of the people threw parties at their homes for the company. One of the parties was at Charlotte Greenwood's home. She invited my wife and me. We were sitting by the pool when Lew Schreiber, who was second in command to Mr. Zanuck walked in. Charlotte was under contract to Fox. I guess she'd invited Zanuck, although I had never worked there. I did not know the hierarchy, but I did know Lew Schreiber. Even though he was very excitable, he was a very nice guy. He was so excitable that many times he would start jumping up and down in his office and end up in the chandelier!

Lew asked me what I was doing.

"Nothing right now. I've been with Paramount."

He said, "Why don't you come to see me at the studio? You should be with us."

That sounded great. Fox was a beautiful studio, was close to where I lived, and I went over to see him the next day. He asked me why I wasn't at Paramount anymore, and I told him the whole story about Henry Ginsburg.

He said, "I'll have to find something for you." I was a little annoyed because I thought he had something definite for me.

He said, "You were in the talent department at Paramount and we don't have a talent department, but you're an experienced assistant director. Would you come in here as an assistant director and gradually work yourself up to something?"

I said that would be fine. Somehow or other Lew and Mack Gordon, who was also a friend of mine that worked at Fox, got to Zanuck and one of the production guys, and when I got home there was a call from the studio. I went to see a man, who said he had a job for me in Arizona. "We have to do some added scenes on *Thunderbirds.* Could you handle it?"

I said, "Of course I can handle it."

He said, "You're hired," and when I said I would not work for scale they gave me a good deal.

Before even seeing Lew or saying "thank you," I was on my way to Arizona, and I was there about three weeks. It was one of those things where the director had said he didn't need a sandstorm, and when he got there he said he did need one. I had to go to the Air Force and borrow a plane, turn it around and use the propeller for a wind machine. That all came back to the studio.

ATKINS: That was another William Wellman film.

JACOBSON: That's right. He had made the picture, but he wasn't there when I went to Arizona. There was another director who did the retakes, and added scenes, Al Werker.

Because they liked the way I handled the work in Arizona, they immediately threw me into the big picture they had coming up, *Crash Dive.*

The director on *Crash Dive* was Archie Mayo. Tyrone Power was the star, and he was a great guy to work with. It was a tough picture to make, because when you're working in a submarine there's not much room. Some of the picture was shot in New London, Connecticut, and the rest of it on the backlot. We had a whole submarine mockup built on the stage, and it worked, because the sets were built for making movies. You could take the side walls out. I loved working on *Crash Dive*.

ATKINS: Tell me about *Jane Eyre*.

JACOBSON: There's a lot to tell about *Jane Eyre*, inasmuch as there was a man named Orson Welles.

David O. Selznick was going to make *Jane Eyre*. He had Joan Fontaine under contract and he had a deal with Orson Welles. He had a whole production layout made by one of the great architects, Bill Pereira. He also had George Barnes, the cameraman. Then for some reason he decided not to make it.

Fox wanted to make it, so Zanuck bought it kit and caboodle from Selznick. That included the script, the cameraman, Orson Welles, Joan Fontaine, and the director, Robert Stevenson.

When I was assigned to the picture I was called in to the production manager's office, who said, "We'd like you to break down the biggest picture we're going to make this year, and tell us how long you think it will take to make, and between you and Ben Silvey, the unit manager, how much it will cost." Fortunately there were no locations. We came up with a sixty-six day schedule.

The production manager blew his top. He said, "We can't afford it. What can we do to make it cheaper?"

I said, "There's only one way to make it cheaper. You'll have to get cheaper stars. You can't afford Orson Welles or Joan Fontaine. Either that or you'll have to cut the script."

They tried to do that and couldn't. The writer got sick, went to the hospital, and was in the hospital all through the picture.

Orson Welles was the associate producer. I went to Orson first thing, introduced myself, and we hit it off. There were a few times when he got a little difficult, but he always came through. For instance, when he played Mr. Rochester in *Jane Eyre,* he wanted to be strong, with the flowing robes. He decided to have a Roman nose. He looked like a baby, with a little pudgy face and a tilted nose. He had this wild make-up man with him all the time, who improvised this nose that baked on to his face in the morning. After it was baked on, they put make-up over it. It took two-and-a-half hours every morning to get him ready.

He lived at the studio, in a bungalow with a bedroom and bath.

To give you an idea of how you worked with Orson Welles — I made arrangements, based on experience, to give him his next day's call in quadruplicate. I gave him a piece of paper with the call on it, showing everything he needed: the page in the script, the scene numbers, the costume he was going to wear, what time he would start and when we expected to finish with him. The second copy went to his secretary. The third was clipped to his script, and the fourth went to me. That way, there would be no doubt about the call.

One morning he walked in fully attired, with the great capes and whatnot. We were going to do the scene where he walked up the stone steps to his crazy wife in the tower. We had a lot of extras milling around in the yard below. He could never whisper — if he whispered, you could hear it on Pico Boulevard.

He called me over and said, "Pray tell, Mr. Jacobson, what are we doing? What are those steps?"

I said, "The scene going up the steps."

He said, "There's no such scene in the script. That was cut out a long time ago."

I said, "Mr. Welles, I respectfully request that you look at the script. It's in there and we're ready to shoot it."

He said, "This is ridiculous that you should call me for this." He was really indignant.

I suggested that he watch his words, and that while we got something else ready, he should sit down and explain to himself and whomever else why he didn't want to do the scene. I called his secretary and couldn't find her. I called my assistant, who kept a copy of the call in his pocket. He was off having a drink somewhere. It was just one of those moments when I was all by myself with my back to the wall. But eventually I found the secretary, and she showed him the call. Meanwhile, the company was smelling blood. He looked at the paper and said, "Well, I'll be damned. How could I make such a mistake?"

I said, "Oh, we all do. Now, can we get on with the scene?"

He said, "No. First, bring me the microphone and loudspeaker." Then he said, "Ladies and gentlemen of the ensemble, will you gather around, please? Can you hear me?" Everybody laughed at that. "I don't know if you noticed that Mr. Jacobson and I were having a slight discussion for the last twenty minutes, but I want to tell you that Mr. Jacobson was right and I was wrong, and I am a horse's ass. I apologize to you publicly."

I said, "That isn't necessary. Let's get on with the work!"

Every once in a while he would do something for radio, and everybody had to clear the stage, except the workers and me. It was fascinating to watch him work for radio. That voice of his would play like a symphony orchestra.

We became friends, and remained so. We used to play little practical jokes on each other. I got home at about seven o'clock one night, after shooting until about six. When I walked in my wife said, "Where have you been all afternoon?"

I said, "I've been working. We just finished."

She said, "That's strange. Orson Welles called and wanted to talk to you, and he said you had finished shooting at three o'clock this afternoon."

I never did convince her that I hadn't been working, but when I saw him the next day I never said a word about it. Another time he invited my wife and me to his home for a party. My wife was five-foot-one. He opened the front door, took one look at her and said, "How can a pretty little thing like you be married to a jerk like that?"

She said, "Don't you say that."

He said, "Oh, come on in and have a drink." He was that kind of fellow.

When we were in Paris making *Little Boy Lost* about ten years later, my wife and I were walking on the Champs Elysées, and at the end of the block was quite a crowd being exhorted by a voice. Whose voice? Orson was making a speech. I don't know what it was about. But I walked through the crowd, got behind him, and kicked him right in the can. He swung around and said, "Oh, no, not you again."

We had a hell of a time for the rest of that evening. He was a great guy.

ATKINS: Since Welles was producing and acting in *Jane Eyre,* how much did Robert Stevenson have to say?

JACOBSON: Nobody could argue with Bob. He was so kind. He was so quiet and easy. There was only one thing that happened. That was when David O. Selznick visited the set. Selznick said "hello" to everyone, and sat down in a chair.

We did a scene, and he called Welles over. Well, you don't call Welles over — if you want to talk to Welles you meet him halfway. But David was used to calling people. I was standing with Welles. Selznick suggested that when they originated this whole thing, the scene they had just played was going to be done a different way. Bob Stevenson was smart and stayed away from these two giants.

Orson said, "No, David, I think we'll just let it go the way it is." He did not subject Bob Stevenson to the embarrassment of saying, "What do you think, Bob?"

David said, "I think you're wrong, Orson."

Orson said, "All right. Artie, let's do it again." He didn't say, "Let's do it again," to Bob.

Bob went through the whole ritual of "speed, roll 'em, action."

Instead of playing the scene, Orson looked right smack into the camera and said, "Ladies and gentlemen, we have a visitor on our set today. His name is David O. Selznick. This is his baby and he feels that the scene should be played in the following manner, not the way we just played it. So here goes."

He played it David's way. I turned around and Selznick was so embarrassed that he was purple. By the time we got through and said, "Cut," David was gone. Then Orson said, "Well, I guess we won't be bothered with that again." Welles could be very cruel.

In addition to his dressing room bungalow, Orson also had an office in the administration building at Fox, because he was a producer. He was all over the place. He called me up to his office the day we finished the picture. He said, "I like you. We get along fine. I'd like you to become the major-domo of my company, Mercury Productions."

I said, "This is a gag, isn't it?"

He said, "No, I'm serious." Then he said that the job would involve a lot of travel, and asked me if I had anything that would tie me down. I explained that travel would be no problem. He told me about his plans to go to South America and do several things there.

I said, "Before we do anything else, can we talk a little bit about a thing called money?"

He said, "No, let's not talk about that." I said, "Now wait. I'm not one of your Mercury players. You're asking me to give up a steady job with a major company, around the corner from my home, to go traipsing all over the world. I expect a lot of money, and — if I may say, Orson — based on your reputation, I also expect the money to be deposited in escrow in a California bank, so I can draw my salary each week."

He said, "We'll work that out in some way."

I said, "What else?"

He said, "If we're going to South America, you'll have to learn a smattering of Spanish and Portuguese."

I said, "Is that all I have to do?"

He said, "No, there's one other thing you have to do. You have to learn to speak English, you son of a bitch."

That's the story. It never came to pass. But I was flattered.

ATKINS: Did you have anything to do with Bernard Herrmann, who wrote the music for the picture?

JACOBSON: No. Within two days after production was finished, I was on another picture. Many times I was preparing the next picture at home at night. That's how busy we were.

One thing about *Jane Eyre,* it was not a smash hit. In my opinion, it was a hell of a fine picture and had great photography, but when the scenes with the little kids were over, which was before the scenes where Fontaine came in, the best part of the picture was over. From there on, it was fine, but it wasn't the picture it should have been.

The three kids were great: Peggy Ann Garner, Elizabeth Taylor, and Margaret O'Brien. There were some great scenes while the kids were in it. One was when the Taylor kid died and Peggy Ann Garner sat with her and held her hand. Another was when they cut Liz's hair off.

When Margaret O'Brien and Orson Welles were in scenes together, she looked about one-and-a-half inches tall, as his shoes were built up and he wore these long, swirling capes. We had scenes where they walked down these corridors with the camera preceding them, and he would just flip a wrist and cover her up with the cape. You couldn't even see her.

ATKINS: I think *Happy Land* may have been made before *Jane Eyre*.

JACOBSON: Yes, it was. I think that was the second picture I did at Fox. We went to one of the sweetest looking towns I've ever been to, Santa Rosa, in the wine country in Northern California. Don Ameche, Harry Carey, Frances Dee and Ann Rutherford were in it. I think this was the first picture Henry Morgan ever did.

This wasn't a long location, but it was so nice because the local people were nice. They'd invite us over and feed us lemonade and cakes. They were just delightful.

Later on, Hitchcock fell in love with the location. When he did *Shadow of A Doubt*, he went up there with his company. The townspeople were thrilled. The whole town turned out to watch them shoot the first day. The assistant director explained that when he said, "Quiet," they had to be pinpoint quiet, or else it would ruin the sound track. They understood and they were cooperative. Right in the middle of the first take a baby cried in the crowd.

Hitchcock yelled, "Cut," and then moved around in his chair and said, "Destroy the child." That became a famous story.

Happy Land was directed by a wonderful man named Irving Pichel. In the crowd, on the first morning, a Russian woman with her four-year-old child in her arms, was watching. Irving was childless, and he was a big man, about the same size as Walter Matthau. He almost looked like Matthau. He was a good actor, too. He played the district attorney in *American Tragedy*.

He asked the lady if she would mind if the baby sat in his lap while we were shooting. She said, "No."

He wrote a little scene into the story in which he started on the sound of a baby's voice crying, cut to a piece of ice cream on the sidewalk, and panned up to see the child with the empty cone crying. It was a very touching bit.

Pichel fell in love with this child, who was a pianist at four years of age, and spoke Russian and English. When we came back, he sent for them and saw to it that they got an agent.

Orson Welles put her in a picture, as a little German girl. Her name was Natasha. She became Natalie Wood.

ATKINS: How about *The Purple Heart*? Was that the only time you worked with Lewis Milestone?

JACOBSON: There was one other time. I knew him very well, socially, and we were very good friends. There's nothing to tell about *Purple Heart*. It was just a routine picture, but it turned out very well.

Milestone was a damn good director. He worked in a very unorthodox manner. He had been a film cutter, and he would never set foot on the set in the morning without knowing exactly what he was going to do. He knew how he was going to direct, where the camera was going to go, and how he was going to cut the film before it was ever developed.

Before we started shooting, on Saturday and Sunday, we went to the studio — Millie, the cameraman, the script girl, a still man and me. We brought the script, some pieces of cardboard, and what they called a quick-sketch artist, like they have in the police department. Millie would take a specific scene and say, "I want to start on a long-shot, and after we get about thirty-five feet of that, I want to move in to a big head closeup." Meanwhile, the artist was sketching, and by the time Millie got through talking he had six shots drawn out. Then the script girl cut out the scene from the script, pasted it on a cardboard with the sketch, and put it in a thing on wheels.

The next morning when we started to shoot, nobody had to say anything except, "We're going to shoot Scene 26, fellows." Everybody walked over to the thing, picked up 26, and knew exactly what they were going to do, while Millie was rehearsing with the actors. It was different, and he worked very successfully that way.

ATKINS: Did he continue to do that throughout his career?

JACOBSON: Oh, yes.

ATKINS: You talked about directors who shouted. How about Milestone?

JACOBSON: He did not shout — he didn't have to shout. Milestone, in a very quiet tone of voice, could cut you to ribbons with sarcasm. When he said what he had to say, that was it. He'd turn on his heel and walk away, without getting into any kind of discussion or argument.

There was one thing, though. As bright as he was, he said to me one day, "Take this script home, read it, and tell me your opinion in the morning. Zanuck sent it to me and he wants me to make it, and I don't think I should. It's one of those impossible things."

I took it home and in the morning I said to him, "You're crazy. If I had the opportunity to do this script I'd kiss their feet."

He wouldn't do it. He was the fifth director to turn it down. They gave it to a schlock director, a guy who would take any piece of junk they handed him. That was Otto Preminger, and the picture was *Laura*. Preminger made it and it changed his life.

In later years I was called in on an emergency to fill in on *Mutiny on the Bounty,* because the unit manager and assistant director were still in Tahiti. They wired the studio to ask me if I could take over until they got back. I asked who was directing it, and they said Milestone. When he directed *Mutiny,* Millie was a very sick man. He was pretty well shot — he would fall asleep in the chair. Brando gave him a very bad time. I said to him one day, "Millie, why do you take this? Why don't you just go home?"

He said, "Artie, I need the money. As long as I'm here and I report every morning, I will get paid. If I quit they'll stop paying me." I liked him.

ATKINS: How about directors who act out the scene for the actors?

JACOBSON: That's old-fashioned. They stopped doing that a long time ago. But then, I didn't work with all the directors, so maybe there are some who still do that.

ATKINS: The next film you did was *Something for the Boys.*

JACOBSON: That was nothing. The director was a very nice guy, Lewis Seiler.

We had a delightful company, with one exception: Michael O'Shea. To me, spending a day with Michael O'Shea was like spending a day walking on hot coals. The others were great. It wasn't much of a picture. The music was kind of cute, and Nick Castle did a lot of good dances.

Seaton and Perlberg

ATKINS: Was *Diamond Horseshoe* the first film you did with George Seaton and William Perlberg?

JACOBSON: Yes. At a studio like Fox you'd be assigned to a picture, period. There were no formalities — you went up and introduced yourself to the director, if you didn't already know him.

While we were doing *Something for the Boys,* a gentleman, whom I'd never seen in my life, came on the set, and introduced himself as George Seaton, Phyllis Lawton's husband. I knew Phyllis from Paramount, where she'd been a dialogue coach in many pictures that I did.

He said, "I'd love for you to have lunch with me if you have the time, because Phyllis and I talked about it last night, and you're very important in my life right now, and I hope it works out."

I said, "I'll have lunch with you, but we've got twenty minutes. If you come back with me afterwards I'll be working, but we can talk."

We went to lunch, and he told me point-blank, "I have just become a director. I wrote the script for *Song of Bernadette* and a lot of other pictures. I talked to Perlberg and Perlberg talked to Zanuck, and I told them I will not go on writing the stuff unless I can direct it myself. They made me a director. I've written a musical with Betty Grable called *Diamond Horseshoe,* and I'd like very much for you to be my assistant. Phyllis says if I have you as my assistant I will not have to worry about anything except directing."

I said, "That's very sweet of Phyllis, but it doesn't work that way. You have to go to Ray Clune and get me assigned to the picture." He said, "No, that isn't the point. I want you to want to be on the picture with me."

I looked at this guy and said to myself, "This doesn't happen in my life." I said to him, "I'd like to, very much. It will be a pleasure."

He went to Perlberg, who was very strong in those days with Zanuck, and I was assigned. Whatever I had been on, they took me off and put me on the Seaton picture. I'm very pleased and flattered to say that he did depend on me — and why not? He didn't have any experience. We made arrangements, through my suggestion, that they build a set and give us a week's rehearsal. That was unheard of.

I think Perlberg was very friendly towards me because of the way George felt. He had brought George over from Columbia, and I found out in later years that Perlberg was jealous of me. He wanted George all to himself. Phyllis told me this, point-blank.

We started the picture, and had a wonderful time, although we had a little trouble with Grable in the middle. She was a little nervous about a new director, because she knew she couldn't act. Everything worked out fine and we became good friends, all of us.

From that moment on, I was on any picture that George did. No matter what I was doing, they took me off it and put me with George. That did not sit well with the company, as they didn't like directors and assistants to become cronies. Many times a director would ask for something that you could talk him out of, and it wouldn't cost so much. If you were a good friend of his, you helped him get it.

ATKINS: When you have a man who has been a very good writer, and this is his first film as a director, how do you guide him?

JACOBSON: George asked me that. He said, "What shall I do? I'll be very nervous. I know about a camera, but I don't know where to put it."

We had a wonderful cameraman, Ernest Palmer, so I said, "Between the cameraman and myself, we'll help you. Ernie and I will take care of where to put the camera. We'll arrange for the cutter to be on the stage, too, if we need him. You'll have sixty to seventy people on your staff, from grips to actors. The minute you answer any one of them, they'll deluge you with questions. So if they ask you a question that has nothing to do with directing, tell them to talk to me. It's my job to answer them." That's the way it worked.

ATKINS: That would allow him to just direct the actors?

JACOBSON: Yes. I'll give you an idea of what he did. We had a scene in *The Country Girl* which was set in the anteroom of the jail. He wanted to rehearse quite a bit with Grace Kelly, without all the crew on the set. He said, "Can we give everybody five, so they can go out and smoke a cigarette? I'd like to be on the set alone with Grace and you."

He dismissed all the people, and rehearsed from nine in the morning until eleven-thirty, broke for lunch, and that afternoon we shot the scene. It was a great scene. That's directing! But when someone says, "Do we have to move that wild wall?," that's not the director's job.

ATKINS: Was George Seaton's first film any more complicated because it was a musical?

JACOBSON: No. We had Hermes Pan, God bless him, and he had a marvelous staff of Angie Blue and Kenny Williams.

As far as the musical was concerned, George understood immediately that it was just staging the scene. All you have to know is that they will pre-record the musical numbers, and you have to have a pretty good idea of how you're going to stage that scene in order to record the music accordingly.

Some directors wouldn't work that way. For instance, there was Wesley Ruggles. When the three brothers did "Small Fry" in *Sing You Sinners,* they were supposed to be strolling musicians. He had three offstage musicians playing along, and we sweetened it later. Musical directors like Arthur Franklin went crazy with that method, but that's the way Wesley Ruggles did it.

There were many headaches for an assistant director. Before the picture started they decided that they wanted eight beautiful girls to appear, and they searched the country for them. They put eight girls under contract to the studio, and used them specifically in *Diamond Horseshoe* for a number where they represent various desserts. As they came forward there was a trick focus slide so they'd come into a huge closeup, and then as they slid out of frame the next one was already approaching. It was very pretty and very effective.

After the third day of shooting somebody came to me and said, "You've got yourself some trouble." He motioned towards one of the girls and said, "You don't have a teacher here. She is fourteen years old, but she lied and said she's eighteen. You know the laws of California. You are responsible."

I went to George and told him about it. He said, "What'll I do?"

I said, "You don't do a thing. I'll do it."

I confronted the girl, and she started to cry. She was out of the picture, but of course we wanted to keep shooting. Fortunately we had one understudy who was the same size. We called off shooting for the day, because, according to health laws, you were not allowed to take the costume off one girl and put it on another. You had to have it cleaned.

When we started to shoot the next morning, we found that the understudy couldn't get into the special bright green shoes she was supposed to wear. We split the shoes down the back, and that's how we finished the sequence.

Something like that happened on *Jane Eyre*. There is a scene where all the kids are lined up, wearing smocks. The smocks were too tight, so we slit them down the back and put shoelaces in them. This is where Bob Stevenson was wonderful. I asked him to shoot the scene in such a way that you never saw the kids' backs. If he had to turn the camera, the girls turned. Those are the things that you can't plan for when you're sitting up in the office.

ATKINS: *Junior Miss* was released in 1945, almost at the same time as *Diamond Horseshoe.*

JACOBSON: We had to find Fluffy, the pal of Peggy Ann Garner. It happened that Val Davies was a very dear friend of George's. Val had kids and Barbara Whiting used to play with them in their front yard. That's where somebody noticed her and called her to George's attention, and he gave Barbara the part of Fluffy.

ATKINS: How was George Seaton as far as working on the set?

JACOBSON: Oh! The salt of the earth. People would break their necks to try to get on his picture. It was so pleasant and always with humor. He never raised his voice, never. He never had a fight with anybody, because the minute he wanted something that I couldn't handle on the set, all he had to do was whisper in Perlberg's ear, and Perlberg was the strong one. He went to bat and always got what George wanted.

ATKINS: Was he particularly good with children?

JACOBSON: With anybody. He had compassion and understanding.

The best thing I can tell you in answer to your questions is, he had a set party when we finished *Anything Can Happen*. There was an actor in it with a strange name. I can't think of it, but he was a good actor. At the party, he got up and said, "I've been in many pictures and I've worked with many directors. I would like to say something about Mr. Seaton. For the first time, because of the director, I understood what I was doing. He took my part and, like a surgeon, operated on it and opened it up. I could see all the inner workings of the character. After I understood, he closed it and sewed it up."

ATKINS: You also worked on *The Dolly Sisters* in 1945.

JACOBSON: They had to remove the assistant director because he wasn't getting along with people, and there was a feud on the set that was very, very bad. The Dolly Sisters had to wear the same costumes and hairdos, and Betty could be pretty rough when she wanted to be. I don't think there was any love lost between her and June Haver, at least not on Betty's part.

Betty came on the set in the morning and had her hair done. She was the only one on the lot who was allowed to have this done; Zanuck said she could decide on her own hairdos without any tests. Of course, they couldn't do June until they saw Betty, who was being done in a closed room. We were never able to start shooting until eleven o'clock in the morning. We let the office know it but they didn't want to do anything about it. Anyway, I replaced the other assistant director.

ATKINS: You worked on *Colonel Effingham's Raid* and *Smoky*.

JACOBSON: There's nothing much to say about *Colonel Effingham's Raid*.

I worked on the second unit of *Smoky*. Louis King was the director, and Jim Tinling was the director of the second unit. I was told by the office when we went on the road that this guy did a little elbow-bending, and that if he ever got too drunk to work I should take over. I didn't want to do that. I'm not that kind of a guy. I fed him chocolate sodas until he was blue in the face, but this particular day, he wasn't much help.

We needed shots of the parade on its way to the rodeo grounds through the city of Cheyenne, Wyoming. It was a nasty day, and photographically it stank. Our horse, Smoky, who has been lost and is now pulling a dray wagon, hears the parade music. In this scene, he joins the parade. We had a driver on the horse who you couldn't see, and we shot it from up above.

The cameraman said, "It's not going to be good, Artie. It's gray and it's practically raining."

I took it upon myself to get the weather report. They said the next day was going to be beautiful, but by that time it would be over. The parade was only for the one day, and the scene would be no good unless we had all the people lining the streets.

I went up to the announcer's booth, and explained the whole thing to the fellow. He got on the microphone, introduced me, and said, "He's going to ask you to do something, and we of the committee would be very grateful if you would cooperate."

I got on the microphone and I cried, "Would everybody please — if the sun is shining — would everybody please come back tomorrow and line the streets, so we can have a second take?"

Thank God, it was better than the first. When I got back to the studio, Ray Clune said, "I heard about what you did at the parade. Congratulations."

Eventually I had to say to Ray, "With all the things I did, you never gave me a chance to direct."

ATKINS: I was interested in *The Shocking Miss Pilgrim* because of the Gershwin music.

JACOBSON: They tried an experiment. George had the idea that they could sell Betty Grable in a picture without having her take her clothes off. The idea was to go exactly the opposite, and make her very prim. She played the first woman typist in Boston, she was covered from neck to ankle, and she was cute as hell. There was Dick Haymes and music, and Miss Goody Two Shoes. It didn't work.

ATKINS: As I recall, they went to a lot of trouble to get the Gershwin songs.

JACOBSON: Yes. Even that didn't do it.

ATKINS: When I interviewed Harry Warren a few years ago, he used the expression, "Betty Grable got 'uppity.'"

JACOBSON: I can understand him saying that. I hate to tell this story, because I liked her so much. I told you, she was a little worried about George, being a new director, when we did *Diamond Horseshoe*. When we were about a quarter of the way through, she was becoming difficult to get out of her portable dressing room. We never called her until we needed her, but many times we were sitting on our cans for ten or fifteen minutes. One day, I got impatient with my assistant, and I said, "What is going on? Why doesn't she come out?" I went to her door and said, "Betty, for God's sakes, let's go. We've been waiting."

She came stomping out and said, "So I'm fifteen minutes late. Artie, why don't you go down to the office and report it?"

That's all she had to say, in front of the whole company. I realized that she had said that I was a snitch who ran down to the office. My hair stood right on end. I was anything but that kind of a guy — I covered those people up like crazy.

George said, "She had no right to say that. That's very insulting. I'm going to have a talk with her."

I said, "No, I'll go and talk to her." I went to her and she said, "Why the hell don't you leave me alone?"

I said, "Betty, we're working, for Christ's sakes."

They were also having great difficulty with her in the wardrobe department.

A call came from Zanuck's office that when we broke for lunch she was to come to his office along with George Seaton, Charles LaMaire, Mr. Perlberg, and Mr. Nye from the make-up department.

The main point of contention was that she disrupted the organization by unnecessarily insulting the assistant director — namely me. That rolled off Zanuck's back, I'm sure, and didn't bother him one bit. The important thing was that we were losing time. He turned right to her and said, "Betty, I've given you privileges. Now I'm calling a halt. Either you change your whole attitude or we will take you off the picture and put somebody else in." Of course she knew they meant June Haver or Alice Faye. He continued, "Now never mind the tears. Don't ruin your make-up and lose another hour of shooting."

By that time Mr. LaMaire had said that he could not get any fitters to work on her. They went home in tears, because she tore and ripped her costumes.

Anyhow, from that moment on, it was paradise. She changed entirely, became her old self, and it was delightful. We were friends until the day she died.

ATKINS: The movie after that is probably George Seaton's most famous film, *Miracle on 34th Street.*

JACOBSON: Yes, without a question of a doubt. It was the classic film. He carried this story around in his pocket for four years — it was called *The Big Heart.* The original idea came from a professor of English Literature at Ann Arbor, Michigan, who told it to Val Davies. Val Davies told it to George and they put it into screenplay form. Val got an Academy Award for original story, George got one for best screenplay, and Edmund Gwenn got it for best supporting actor.

George was sitting on his "canetta," getting big money as a director, but not working. They were looking frantically for a property for him to direct. He said to me one day at lunch, "I don't know what they're going to give me, but the few things I've come up with they don't want to do. It's an impasse."

I said, "What about *The Big Heart?*"

He said, "Zanuck can't see it."

Finally they said, "Go ahead and shoot it if you can arrange it."

George had been to New York several times over the two preceding years. He had seen Jack Strauss, who was the head of Macy's, and Bernard Gimbel, of Gimbel's. It was all set, but we had to make arrangements for nine cameras on Thanksgiving morning, to shoot the parade. We got there two days ahead of time to shoot the parade.

Various technical things happened at Macy's during the shooting of *Miracle on 34th Street.* For instance, we shot a lot of the stuff at night, with extras. For one scene we wanted to get ten thousand people on the main floor at Macy's. We could shoot from the mezzanine and see way down. We had to light the whole thing at night, and shoot it during the day.

At the last minute, two departments came to us. One was the Department of Safety, who said, "You cannot have these cables on the floor, because people will stumble over them, and there will be lawsuits and injuries."

The Fire Department said, "You cannot hit switches and then have all the bright lights come on, because somebody who's stepping on an escalator will turn around to see what's happened and will trip and fall."

One of the grips came to me and said, "Why don't we take the cables that are on the floor and run them up the pilasters, scallop them along the ceiling, and put Christmas bunting around them?"

We had to put every light on a rheostat and bring them up gradually.

Handling the crowds was part and parcel of the job. Sometimes we were shooting in the cafeteria and we were using the real people from Macy's. We put Edmund Gwenn and the kid in the line with them. These people only had so much time for lunch, so we shot it immediately.

ATKINS: Were cast and crew staying at one hotel?

JACOBSON: No. They were scattered around. The crew lived at the Pennsylvania Hotel because most of our work was at Macy's, which was right around the corner. George always stayed at the Hampshire House. Edmund Gwenn, Natalie Wood, and John Payne stayed there too.

Maureen O'Hara wanted to stay at the Sherry-Netherland. So we put her up there. Her brother, his wife and kid came down from Canada to visit, and they moved right in with her without telling anybody. They were sleeping on the floor in the living room. The hotel management wanted her to take a larger suite or pay for the extra guests, and when she refused they evicted her. We tried to get her into the Hampshire House, but the Hampshire House and the Sherry-Netherland had the same management, so there was a problem. Eventually Maureen got into the Hampshire House — but without her brother and his family.

Maureen learned another lesson. This was Thanksgiving time and you can imagine the mobs Christmas shopping in Macy's. She said to me one day, "Could you get a special officer to walk with me? I want to do some shopping."

I said, "I know New Yorkers. They aren't going to pay any attention to you. Don't wear a bandanna around your head, or dark glasses. Just be normal." I offered to walk with her. Nobody paid a damn bit of attention to her. It broke her heart.

We all got along fine. Johnny Payne was a wonderful guy. Natalie was a dream. Edmund Gwenn was the salt of the earth. So, except for the unit manager, who threw a gloom over the whole thing, it went wonderfully.

The unit manager was an irresponsible guy and should never have been sent on location. It reached a point one day when I said to George, "I'm going home, I can't stand working with this guy."

George went to him very quietly and said, "Stay off the set."

We shot half the picture in Macy's, and came home to finish it. Zanuck didn't even go to the preview. When the cards came in, they were put on his desk the next morning. He read them all, ordered another preview that night, and sure enough, it was a hit.

When the time came for Academy Award consideration for best picture, they had a picture called *Gentlemen's Agreement*, which beat *Miracle on 34th Street* by one vote. Nobody was ever told how to vote. Ha Ha!

ATKINS: Are there people who work well in the studio and not so well on location?

JACOBSON: Oh, yes, yes. A lot of people go on location, forget they're married, shack up with somebody, and forget that they have a nine o'clock call — knowing that there is somebody there that will take their work over for them.

Years before on *The Big Broadcast*, we were in New York for ten days, and the unit manager went there four days before anyone else. It was like letting a hen-pecked guy out of a cage, with all expenses paid.

He shacked up with somebody, and wouldn't tell anybody where he was. We never saw him until the last day of shooting. We covered for him until the bills for the clothes came in, which he should have okayed. He had to explain, which he wasn't able to do.

ATKINS: What about *Thunder in the Valley*?

JACOBSON: That was directed by Louis King. The cameraman was Charles Clarke. I was the assistant director. The unit manager does not deserve to be named. He was on the take, and was eventually thrown out of the business. The cast starred Peggy Ann Garner, Lon McCallister, Edmund Gwenn, Reginald Owen, and a sheep dog, whose name I can't remember.

It was all done on location, in Kanab, Blue Springs, and Panquiche Lake, Utah, except for a few interiors which we did when we got back. Everything was very pleasant except for where the unit manager was concerned, which unfortunately was almost everywhere.

I just wanted to add one thing about *Junior Miss*. The whole story took place in the New Year's season in New York City. Walter Winchell came through one time and said, "How come when they shoot scenes of people in New York City their breath never shows?"

George was a stickler for perfection and realism. When the kids were on the ice rink making all their outlandish plans, George had the crew rig up the most God-blessed thing you ever saw. It ran up the sides of a kid's body, came around, and a little pipe was attached to the kid's face, so that smoke could be pumped through the pipes. Every time the kids talked you saw their breath, if you were shooting from a certain angle. It worked out fine.

ATKINS: You worked on several other films in this period that were not Seaton-Perlberg pictures.

JACOBSON: There were many times when Seaton wasn't going to do a picture for six months. He'd be writing. They weren't going to let me sit on my butt, and I didn't want to sit. They assigned me to *Give My Regards to Broadway,* which was a completely pleasant picture. Lloyd Bacon was a doll. We had Dan Dailey. A lot of people had trouble with him, but because we were very good friends I never did. It was cute, but just another picture.

Chicken Every Sunday was a George Seaton picture, and Dan Dailey was in that, too, along with Celeste Holm and Colleen Townsend. Colleen married a minister, and has been living a beautiful religious life ever since. Natalie Wood played the kid sister in that. But again, it was nothing special.

The Walls of Jericho was a big, ponderous, important picture directed by John M. Stahl. We had a hell of a cast in that thing: Cornel Wilde, Anne Baxter, Kirk Douglas, Linda Darnell, Marjorie Rambeau, Henry Hull, and Colleen Townsend. It was about a small town with big doings.

I just remember one thing. John Stahl was a very rough guy. He was white-haired and very patriarchal, and he always wore dark glasses. It's very difficult to talk to a man wearing dark glasses, because you can never see his eyes. He was the boss — the king of all he surveyed. He had been quite unreasonable all week. We were shooting a garden party on the big crane. We broke for an hour for lunch, but he came back in thirty minutes. I had stayed on the set and had a sandwich sent in. Ten minutes later he said, "Let's go."

I said we couldn't go until all the people got back, and added, "If you had told me, I would have called a half-hour lunch," I reminded him that it took a half-hour to walk to the commissary and back, and promised that at exactly on the hour we would go.

After another ten minutes he started again: "Let's go."

I said, "Come on, Mr. Stahl. Let me do my work." With that I turned and the patch pocket of my brand new tweed jacket caught on the crane and ripped.

I said, "Now, goddamn it, you see — ."

He said, "Don't you talk to me like that."

I said, "Mr. Stahl, let's be reasonable. You're the director. I'm the assistant. I'm trying to do my job. Now let me do it."

I felt somebody grab me by the arm, drag me off the stage, and walk me all around the stage. It was Linda Darnell. She and I were very good friends. She had come back and heard the argument. She said, "I'm saving your job for you, you damn fool. Calm down."

I said, "Don't ask me to apologize."

She said, "I wouldn't ask you to apologize to that old son-of-a-bitch. By the time we get back on the set he will have forgotten about it."

We went back on the set, shot the scene, and that was the last I heard about it to this day.

ATKINS: What do you mean when you say he was "rough"?

JACOBSON: Well, for instance, there was an actor in the picture named Art Baker. He was a great radio announcer. He had white hair, and he looked just like John Stahl. Now Stahl always wanted to be an actor, and he was very jealous of this man. Baker could not satisfy Stahl no matter what he did, until finally he blew up one day, and said, "Mr. Stahl, I suggest that you get another actor. I can't seem to satisfy you. You know what you want, so get somebody else."

Stahl said, "Now take it easy."

Baker said, "I can't take it easy. You won't let me." This is what people used to say to Preminger and Hathaway.

He did another thing that I could never understand. I'd say, "Places," and the actors took their places. Then he'd run through a rehearsal. They'd still be in place, and he'd roll the camera and say, "Speed." Then he'd say, "All right. Now, children, hold. Hold. Hold."

The camera was still going. People stood like statues. Then he'd say, "Now! Give me a lot of energy and — Action!" And they'd play the scene.

I was called down to the front office a couple of times. They said, "What can you do with this man? Do you know how much film is wasted?"

I said to the producer, "Why are you talking to me? Why don't you talk to Mr. Stahl?"

They said, "You find out about it first." He had intimidated them.

When the picture was all finished we were fairly good friends, and I asked him why he did that. He said, "When I was a young director I had my own company called Tiffany-Stahl, down on Vermont Avenue. I also cut the film. One time I got into a bind where I just didn't have enough film at the beginning of the scene, and it was spoiled. From then on I wanted to be sure. But from what you tell me, it has become a bad habit." From then on he never did it again.

Stahl used to brag about one thing. He bet on the races and he usually won six out of eight. We found out later that he bought a ticket on every horse.

ATKINS: I think the next film was *Mr. Belvedere Goes to College.*

JACOBSON: That was with Clifton Webb, Shirley Temple, Alan Young, and Gil Stratton, who was a sports announcer. Elliott Nugent directed that. I did two pictures with him, and I loved him. Elliott was a very quiet, wonderful guy, a brilliant talent. There were no problems, except that, when we were going home, I lost him in the airport, and I finally found him in the men's room. It was the first inkling I ever had that there was something wrong.

He was called in to do a comedy called *Father Was a Fullback.* Something happened to him, I don't know what. He didn't know what he was doing. He was rambling. He lost his equilibrium or some damn thing, and they had to replace him.

Of all people to put on, they used heavy-handed John Stahl. He was a good enough craftsman to follow the script, but I could never see one semblance of humor in him. It was rather embarrassing — the next day, after Stahl came on, Elliott came on the set and watched, went up to Stahl and said, "You're doing it wrong."

We had a hell of a time getting him off the set. I never saw him again. He did *The Male Animal.* He was a good actor, writer and director. He passed away in 1980.

One thing I'd like to add about *Apartment for Peggy* — just a few months before the picture was made, we had a stillborn child, our one and only. We had used George's doctor and hospital, and it was just one of those unfortunate things — my wife never got over it.

George came to me after everything was well — as well as it ever could be — and said, "I have a wonderful scene to play, but I don't want to put it in the picture because when Gloria sees it, it's liable to upset her terribly. So will you talk it over and ask her if it's all right?"

This is the kind of man George was.

Gloria said, "It's fine." The scene was that Jeanne Crain had a stillborn child. Bill Holden walked out of the hospital room, went down to the street outside and walked with Edmund Gwenn, a brain who knew everything. Bill Holden stopped and asked the professor, "Why?" The professor said, "I don't know."

When you saw it in the movie, it did things to you. That's the way George worked.

It was a good picture. Jeanne Crain was anything but a great actress. George made a fine actress out of her, because she had things to say, words and words and words. She never stopped. She was like a chatterbox when she talked to the old man. When I read the script I asked George, "How are you going to get her to do this?"

He said, "I don't know, but I'm going to try."

When he got her to do it, I said, "How did you do it?" He showed me the script again, and pointed out that there was no punctuation in the long speeches. One word ran right into another, no commas, no periods, no pauses. Sure enough, it worked. It was a trick of his.

ATKINS: You worked on *I Was a Male War Bride,* directed by Howard Hawks in 1949.

JACOBSON: I loved him! Howard Hawks had a great sense of humor, but he would never belly-laugh. He'd smile a little. I just loved working with him. He was the kind of man who never said, "Boo." You had to read his thoughts. Sometimes we wouldn't shoot a scene until eleven o'clock in the morning, and at three in the afternoon we were finished with the day's work and went home. He knew what he wanted.

Working with Ann Sheridan was paradise. We had met on one of those early pictures, *Search for Beauty,* I think. We got to be great friends. Oh, what a sense of humor that gal had. She laughed like a drunken full-of-beer truck driver.

Cary Grant was a pleasure to work with. He was especially fun in the scene where he had to wear a wig.

ATKINS: What about *Love That Brute*?

JACOBSON: It had been made before. I can't think of the title of the original. Paul Douglas played a gangster who was saddled with a little boy who wasn't a little boy, but a mean little gangster.

Al Hall was the director. I had worked with him before, and he was fine. I'd known him for years. He was a film cutter. I think he did the original version of *Little Miss Marker.* But he did a little elbow-tipping. I think he's gone now. They nicknamed him after the old vaudevillian, Al K. Hall, alcohol. But he was a marvelous comedy director.

Jean Peters was playing the lead in the picture. She had just won a Miss Ohio beauty contest, and right off the bat she became a leading lady. She was just a natural. She was a beauty and she could act.

ATKINS: Was *For Heaven's Sake* the last thing you did at Fox?

JACOBSON: Yes, but before that was *I'll Get By,* which was just a typical musical. William Lundigan was the lead.

Richard Sale, the director, had been a writer for a long time with his wife, Mary Loos, who, in turn, was Anita Loos' niece. They still worked as a team. He went over to Europe and made a picture, something along the lines of *The Dolly Sisters.*

George Seaton wrote the original story for *For Heaven's Sake.* Clifton Webb played an angel, and God sent him down to Earth to try to get this couple to give birth to a baby, but they were too busy putting on Broadway shows. Another angel, Edmund Gwenn, was sent down to look out for Mr. Webb, and there was a lot of fun between them. Mr. Webb became visible to the couple and in one scene he started playing the harp that's in their living room. He played a wonderful jazz harp number.

Clifton Webb was the kind of actor who said to George three months before the picture went into production, "If I'm going to play the harp, I'm going to play the harp. We are not going to have somebody else's fingers do it. I want you to be in a position at my feet and not cut to me, but to pan to me, and then pull away so you see my face. I want the audience to see that I'm playing."

They put him in the hands of one of the great jazz harpists, Maxwell Rosen, whose professional name is Robert Maxwell. Clifton worked with him five days a week, and by the time we were ready to shoot the scene he played the number. It was like learning a part by rote.

The important thing about *For Heaven's Sake* is my admiration, as people and as actors, of Clifton Webb — and Edmund Gwenn.

Foreign Locations

JACOBSON: Because I had been abroad many times and always did a good job, I became the guy that they sent abroad. I could work on my own. As I said, when George was writing, I didn't sit around, I was given other assignments.

In 1948, they said, "A French director, Julien Duvivier, is here, and he's under contract to Alexander Korda of London Films. He feels that he can make a fine picture in Tahiti, about one of the heroes down there, and he feels that he can make it very reasonably."

Korda said that he couldn't afford to make the picture by himself, but arrangements could be made for them to go down there if they could do a co-production on it, with Duvivier directing, Korda putting up a certain amount of money, and Twentieth Century-Fox furnishing the rest of the money, the equipment, and the manpower with the know-how. The country was all French. If you're an American you've got to get all sorts of permits to get in there. Ray Clune showed me the letter that Zanuck had received from Korda. Zanuck had scribbled across it, "Send your best man and bring back a report." I was the best man.

I introduced myself to Duvivier, who sat behind a big desk. He reeked of perfume and held a long cigarette holder. He was a typical Frenchman. I could see that he was used to having people do things for him, but I never did kowtow to directors.

He told me the plan, which was to stop in Honolulu for a week on the way to Tahiti, to make tests of girls in case we couldn't find them down below. He had done some research and had heard that there were some very attractive women in Tahiti, but that they had bad teeth, et cetera.

After we made 16-millimeter tests in Hawaii we'd go to Nandi, in Fiji, at which time we'd get away from Pan American. Duvivier had a friend who owned a small airline which was based in New Caledonia. One of his planes was going to pick up Duvivier, his wife, my wife and myself. We didn't know how long we'd be there — maybe a month, maybe six months.

We had to do our work, go back to the studio with our report, and then go back to Tahiti to shoot the picture before the monsoon season started.

We had a little run-in in Honolulu, when he wanted me to take his wife's coat to a storage place. I had explained in so many words that I was a production man from Twentieth Century-Fox, not a mere gofer or ass-kisser who could be ordered around. We had an understanding after that.

Our plane was supposed to arrive the morning after we got to Nandi. They put us up in a military structure, which had a thatched roof, a single bulb hanging down, army cots, and a main dining room with blue-black waiters, without shoes. Between everything they did they played one record over and over. We sat and listened to it, stoically. Unfortunately, the airplane from New Caledonia didn't arrive the next morning. There were no telephones except through military radio-telephone. We weren't able to make contact with New Caledonia.

We were stuck there for about a week, and I thought this Frenchman was going to go absolutely out of his mind. At dinner he ordered wine. There was no such thing.

Another week went by, and it was raining all the time. He was becoming a nervous wreck. His wife was no help. She was a countess, or something. My wife could rough it.

We met some New Zealanders, who went out on boats. Madame Duvivier wouldn't go. Finally we found out that a hurricane had hit New Caledonia, and the airline's three planes had been destroyed. We had to decide whether to go back to Hollywood, which we could do on Pan American, or find another way to get to Tahiti. There were no airplanes to Tahiti in 1948. There was some talk about going there by boat. The people asked an astronomical figure to take us there and back.

I cabled Clune and told him the whole story. I recommended that the studio not spend what was being asked for the boats. I also said, "I haven't any idea what we are going to run into when we get to Tahiti. Duvivier claims he doesn't need any equipment, and that with six lights we'll be able to do the whole thing. It doesn't hold water."

He said, "Use your own judgment."

ATKINS: Did you have a studio cameraman?

JACOBSON: No. He was going to bring the cameraman from England. This was a Korda, London film. That's why we were being allowed in. I didn't know it at the time, but Duvivier had an assistant in England who he was going to bring down, along with a cameraman. This assistant had lost his job because when Korda found out about me, he didn't carry the other guy. So without my knowing it, there were two strikes against me, because Duvivier had to tell his assistant, "I'm sorry, but they've saddled me with an American jerk." Those are my words.

Finally we contacted a small company in Sydney, Australia, that owned a four-engine Sunderland converted bomber that had been used by the Australian Air Force during the war. They gave us an estimate based on so many idle hours, taxiing hours and flying hours. After a lot of wrangling, we made a deal for them to take us to Tahiti, drop us off, and take us back to Nandi thirty days later. They would be paid a blanket fee of $17,000 when we returned to our starting point. If we did not return, it was just too bad for them. We found out later that the pilot had never flown from Fiji to Tahiti.

We'd moved to a hotel on the main island of Fiji. The plane arrived, and our little captain, president of the company, came to me. He was a real Australian. He threw me a salute, because I was the boss and in charge of the money. He said there would be a slight delay because some minor repairs had to be made, but after a delay of forty-eight hours we took off. The plane stopped in British Samoa for refueling. The refueling process was done by bringing a motor-boat filled with oil drums out to where the plane was anchored, and hand-pumping in the oil.

We took off, but were losing our daylight, so we stopped in the Cook Islands. They didn't want us, because there had been an epidemic. We finally got to Tahiti, where we stayed for thirty days. On the thirtieth day I couldn't wait for that airplane to get there. I was so tired of it.

First of all, we found the queen's castle, which was a frame building three stories high and at least a hundred yards wide, with about a hundred windows. Duvivier's idea was for a party scene, where we'd start on the porch and pull back amongst the crowd, with all the windows lit. He was very enthusiastic and said, "The studio has more lamps."

I said, "Yes, but you have told them you could do this on a shoestring."

We went to Moorea. There was no way to get there except in a small boat. To get our equipment in, we would have had to build a pier. There was no place to live. We would have had to build a camp. We found out that the electric power fluctuated, which meant we'd have to bring in our own generators.

The airplane came back, and we went back to Fiji. We lost an engine. We found out much later — it took seven years to settle the suit — that the viscosity, the weight, of the oil they had put in the plane on the second trip down was incorrectly marked, and consequently it got so thin that it tore out a piece of one of the cylinders.

The pilot started skimming the water, trying to land without hitting the coral. It didn't take long before we lost a second engine, and down we went. We had just enough time to try to put on our life-jackets, which had never been used. They were filthy, but we put them on anyhow. We did all the things you're supposed to do, taking our shoes off and so on. He hit the water. As a kid, I remember taking a flat rock and spinning it across a lake. It would bounce! That's how he landed that airplane. We only had two engines left. He brought the plane down and let the tail hit, then gunned it a little and let the tail hit again, shortening it each time. Finally we were floating, five miles from land. We were in British Samoa.

It didn't take long before you saw all the canoes coming out to us, and one long-boat with a white man in it. He was a pharmacist's mate from the United States Navy at Pago Pago, serving a year's hitch as the doctor to the natives on the island. There were seventeen people aboard the plane, ten of us, and some people we had allowed Duvivier to bring to defray some of the expenses. That night we killed chickens and fried them, used the one shower that they had, and sent a MAYDAY for the Navy to come and rescue us.

They took us to the governor's mansion in British Samoa, and we stayed there for five days while they tried to repair the airplane. The governor lived in Robert

Louis Stevenson's home, which we found very interesting. Finally they repaired the plane, flew back to Fiji and paid off the pilot of the plane who had saved our lives.

Duvivier collapsed with a complete nervous breakdown. We had to get a doctor, and were stuck there a few days, but at last we were able to fly to Honolulu. Paradise! There had been stories in all the newspapers that we had been lost at sea, drowned. I said, "Oh, I never thought of that. My mother, in New York —."

Sure enough they were mourning my wife and myself. I called my boss from Honolulu. He said, "Can you get out of there in a day or so?"

I said, "I am so shot and so nervous, I don't want to get into an airplane. Give me five days."

He said, "Get on a plane day after tomorrow."

Instead I stayed there for five days and didn't answer the phone. I had a ball, at Twentieth's expense.

Then I went home, wrote my report, took it up to Duvivier a week after I arrived in Hollywood, and showed it to him. It was very thick, and it was a completely honest report. When I took the report to Ray Clune, he looked at and said, "I want you, in one sentence, to tell me what your opinion is."

I said, "If you put a nickel into this project you should have your head examined. Whatever you do, it's going to get worse and worse, and the money is going to mount."

Apparently he called Zanuck, and Zanuck called the whole thing off. Duvivier didn't know this. Zanuck had not yet gotten in touch with Korda in London.

When I gave Duvivier the report he took it home, and the next morning, he gave it back to me and said, "Have it rewritten with all my notes on the margins."

I read the margins. I said, "I'll have another report written, signed by you. We'll put two reports in."

He said, "No, no, no. Just sign the one."

I said, "No. You're talking to me as if I'm a hayseed. Everything you've written in this report is a lie. No dice."

We fell out. He went back to Europe. But there's a coincidence. I was in Berlin, working on *The Big Lift*. One evening I was waiting for the elevator. It opened, and out stepped Julien Duvivier and his wife. "Hello." That's all. Sometime later I was in Rome and we went to a restaurant we'd heard about. We sat down, and in two minutes a couple came in and sat at another table facing us. It was Duvivier and his wife. We went to England and ran into them again. It turned out that his wife had cancer, and they were running to all the doctors in Europe, which was why we were running into him every place. Next thing we knew she died, and about a year after that he died.

I don't recall the name of the picture he was supposed to make, or the name of the hero it was supposed to be about.

ATKINS: There is some disagreement in some of the screen credit books about who released *The Big Lift*.

JACOBSON: It was Twentieth Century-Fox. George Seaton wrote the script. Seaton and Perlberg were strong enough to get what they wanted, and they wanted me on every picture they made. I was called into the office and told that my next assignment was to go to Germany with George on *The Big Lift*.

George said we would be gone about seven months. He was going to finish the script in Germany, where everything was happening, and while he was writing, we would have a camera crew from Hollywood doing airplane second unit work. It was the end of the airlift into Berlin.

At first I told Ray Clune that I wouldn't be able to go because of the studio's rule against taking wives along. I said, "I'd understand if I was going to be sharing a tent with someone, but I'm sure I'll be in a hotel in Berlin, and I'm willing to pay for my wife's transportation and room."

He said the wives would be distracting.

I said, "On the contrary. When your wife is there you don't go carousing around."The studio refused to let her go, so I didn't go. They put me on a picture called *The Gunfighter,* with Henry King, but nothing ever came of that.

George left with the unit manager and an assistant director, and they were there for months doing all this stuff. They started to shoot right on the apron at Templehof, which was a busy place, because each time an airplane came in full of cargo, a truck backed into it as it taxied to a stop. The minute the stuff was loaded into the truck, the plane taxied away and took off. This happened every three minutes, around the clock. It was a fantastic operation.

After a week, all hell broke loose. George wasn't satisfied with the assistant director, and the unit manager was too busy making arrangements. Sunday morning rolled around, and my telephone rang. It was George, calling from Berlin. He said, "I don't want to talk to you. I want to talk to Gloria."

He got Gloria on the phone, and she listened and listened. Finally, she turned to me and said, "George needs you. He's in great trouble. And it's all right with me if you go."

They called Henry King and told him that George needed me. Henry said to me, "Our dear friend George is in trouble. They want you to get on your horse and get over there right away. Clune called me to find out if it would interfere with my picture. I told him I don't need you. I've made a lot of pictures without you. George is a neophyte and I'm an old man. So they'll give me somebody. Get over there."

They wanted me to go to Berlin, arrive on Sunday and go to work on Monday morning. Instead of firing the other guy, they were going to give him another job of some kind, a liaison between this and that.

My passport was always in order. They sent me from Hollywood to New York, and then by plane from New York to Paris, because they did not have my military permit into the American sector of Berlin, and they wanted me to get it in Paris. It was very nice, because I got stuck in Paris for two or three days while waiting for them to do what they had to do.

I was to go to Frankfurt and then to Berlin. Instead of sending me into Frankfurt by air they sent me by train. Things were still hot. Most of the people on the train were German, and there were no smiles. There was the Jewish question and all, and I felt very strange getting in the train all by myself, with a big beautiful overcoat and two suitcases. I looked like I had a couple of bucks.

I was supposed to be met at nine o'clock in the morning when the train arrived in Frankfurt by a public information officer. I got off the train. You know how they put your suitcases through the window? There was nobody there to meet me. So there I stood with my two suitcases and my long tweed coat, feeling like a sore thumb amongst all these people. It was the same time that all the Germans were coming in to go to work, and they were too busy even to notice me. Finally the station emptied.

I picked up the two suitcases and went to the baggage room. In my broken German, and trying to keep my Jewish accent out of it, I put enough authority into my voice so that the guy wouldn't argue with me. I wanted to put the suitcases there until I found my destination. I went out onto the street, and stopped the first G.I. I saw. I asked, "Where is the Park Hotel?" This is where the company was staying.

He said to go down a block, turn, and go down another block. I did what he told me, but there was no hotel. I retraced my steps, and decided not to ask another G.I. An officer came by, and I asked him. He said the hotel was right across the street.

I went in and found the guy who was supposed to meet me. He was a captain, he had a hangover, and he was sitting at his desk in a bathrobe. I introduced myself, and he said, "Oh, my God! I forgot to meet you."

Later I went to the airport where I met a colonel, who took me to lunch. Finally I had a military transport, and we started to go through the process to get me on the plane to Berlin. A young sergeant looked at my papers. He said, "The papers are not in order, sir."

The colonel tried to persuade him, but the sergeant kept refusing. We found out that the reason my papers were not in order was because on the back side of each piece of paper was a duplicate in Russian. The sergeant said, "If this plane should ever come down in any Russian territory, this man could be incarcerated for life and nobody would ever know what became of him."

The colonel apologized to the young man, I got on the plane, and sure enough the cameraman was there. He had come to meet me.

When I got to Berlin, it was all hugs. George said, "Stay with us tonight, have dinner, and I'll fill you in on everything."

I said, "I've got a pretty good hunch because I know the assistant you have."

He said, "Well, he sits down all the time. These Germans have to be told what to do, and they'll do it. But you can't treat them gently." But before we do anything, I want you to get something out of your system. I did it. I want you to do it. I'm going to take you to the location where we're shooting tomorrow morning."

It was a drizzly afternoon. We got out of the car, and he got back in. He said, "I'll leave you alone. I just want you to look around. I'll be back in five minutes."

It was complete rubble. There was a terrible smell. I think to this day there are decaying bodies there. All of a sudden, something hit me and I started to cry. I sat down on the curb and cried like I had never cried in my life. I could see the whole thing happening. You could hear it; you could hear the screams. You've never seen such rubble.

We went to the house, the billet they called it. Phyllis was there with her two kids and a nurse. Montgomery Clift had brought a gal over. The business of wives not going was ridiculous. If you came out of Zanuck's office you could do anything you pleased, but if you came out of Clune's office you had to abide by his rules.

We were going to do a sequence with trains in the subway. There was a hiring hall in Berlin where you could get extras, and the ones that they sent were well-dressed — the elite of extras. George said, "That isn't what I want. My God, I wanted them the way they really are."

We dismissed them and the next morning, at seven o'clock, we went outside the subway, with our German assistant. We promised people so many marks if they'd stay with us and make movies all day. We just took them right off the sidewalk. They didn't know what was going on. All they knew was that they were going to get so much money. That's the way we made that picture, and it was all right.

ATKINS: Was any of this picture made in Hollywood?

JACOBSON: No. It was all done in Germany. We had a small studio in the American sector. If we did anything here, they were added scenes later. We had two German actresses. One played the lead, and it didn't take long before she and I tangled. One windy day we were working, and we called for her hairdresser. They said the hairdresser was in a bier-stube, across the square. I went across the square, got her, and said, "Unless you get on the set right now, you're through."

The leading woman found out about it. She started on me, and we had it out right there on the sidewalk. She tried to extract everything from the company she could. We finally realized that she was really a Nazi.

Another thing happened that was very significant. We did a scene in front of a bakery, and we had about a hundred extras lined up to buy half a loaf of bread. Without realizing that the extras could hear what I was saying, I said to my assistant, Lloyd Allen, "Isn't this fantastic, what one country can do to save a city from starving to death?"

This was not only a scene we were playing, it was the real thing. One of the German extras turned to me and said, "And why not? Look what you did to us."

That was the end of that. I never even answered him. As far as they were concerned, there was no reason why we had to go in and destroy a city.

ATKINS: The studio you mentioned: was that something that had not been demolished, or did they build it?

JACOBSON: It was a little studio in the American sector, and that section of Berlin had not been demolished. What had been shattered was the great Brandenburg Gate, with all the statues. If statues hadn't been damaged by bombs, then noses and arms were knocked off by the soldiers.

We did work at the Brandenburg Gate. They told us that anything we had to take to the East German side of the gate must be expendable. We could not come back with it. They were liable to take it away from us, even though we had the British okay, and the British had the German-Russian okay.

The minute we'd say, "Action," radios would start to play all around the place to destroy our scene and ruin the sound track. We did an old trick — we reversed the whole thing. We rehearsed the scene, and then we said, "Action." The rehearsal was actually being shot. The boy with the microphone had a long pole, so the mixing panel could be on the other side of the Brandenburg Gate. It was a little touchy to shoot that way.

One time we were all sitting on a parallel, waiting for the weather to break. The cameraman was sitting there with his hat down over his head. The next morning the Communist paper from East Germany came out with a picture on the front page. They said, "The American film moguls at work," and it looked as if we were all asleep. That's the way it was.

ATKINS: I won't go into all the political ramifications, but you did feel there were still lots of Nazis?

JACOBSON: Oh, yes. We used a Mercedes-Benz that was supplied by the Air Force. We had a driver who spoke no English. Willi was his name. When the shooting was over, he drove us home for the last time.

I invited him in. We got everything we wanted at the PX, a bottle of Pinch Bottle Haig and Haig for five bucks, that sort of thing. I gave him a bottle of that for his going-away gift. He said in his broken English that on every holiday he would have one glass, to make it last.

I said, "Sit back, Willi. We're just people here. You're not a servant. Just relax." I said to the hausfrau, "Give Willi a drink."

He hadn't had a drink of Scotch in God knows how long. I could see the hausfrau in the background doing something. She didn't think it was a good idea, because he was going to drive home. By the time he had his third drink you could see little patches of pink coming in his cheeks. He was really leaning back and getting very comfortable.

I said, "You weren't in the war, were you?" I threw it at him.

He didn't stand up but he straightened up and he said, "I was captain in the Afrika Korps."

There were no Nazis. There were no German soldiers ever, anywhere. Jewish — they never heard of it. They said, "If it was, it was military." Everybody was military.

ATKINS: That film wasn't released until 1950.

JACOBSON: We made it in 1948. I don't know if there was any reason for the long time in between.

Return to Paramount

ATKINS: You left Twentieth Century-Fox and went to Paramount sometime after *The Big Lift.*

JACOBSON: I went with Perlberg and Seaton because I was included in their deal when they went to Paramount in 1951. However, as I told you, I lived up to my vow that I would never set foot in any studio where Henry Ginsburg was.

ATKINS: I think the first picture you worked on there was *Rhubarb.* Officially you were "Assistant to the Producers."

JACOBSON: Right. Seaton and Perlberg produced that picture, but Arthur Lubin directed it. There were quite a few pictures that they produced which George didn't direct, because he was busy writing.

We had a lot of fun on *Rhubarb.* We made that picture in a very economical, intelligent way. Arthur Lubin was used to working with animals. He had done all the Francis the Talking Mule pictures, and later did *Mr. Ed.* Arthur was a young actor playing a Parisian gigolo when I first knew him him in 1926. I met him again in London when he was doing a picture called *Footsteps in the Fog,* with Jean Simmons and Stewart Granger.

There's no such thing as a trained cat. A cat will do all kinds of tricks in its own living room, but when you get it in a studio living room and turn on the lights, it goes right to sleep. Wherever we needed shots of the cat by itself, we skipped them, and wherever the cat was with actors, Arthur shot it. When we finished, we looked at the picture and said, "Insert missing shot in which the cat does so and so."

With the help of Frank Inn, the animal trainer, who was just breaking in, but has since won a Patsy award and become a millionaire, I took the second unit, and directed all the cat scenes. Some of the things we did with that cat were fantastic. I was known at Paramount as the "pussy director," and my office became the "cat house." You know, nice people we have in this business.

In the story, Rhubarb the cat inherited a baseball team — a superstitious bunch who thought the cat brought them good luck if they touched it before they played in a game. Gangsters who were betting on the World Series kidnapped the cat on the last day. The game was being played at Ebbets Field in Brooklyn, while the cat was chained up in a hotel room in New York.

Rhubarb wanted to get to the game and cleverly slipped off her collar. The SPCA man told us how to accomplish this, saying, "It's very simple. It won't hurt the cat. Just put one drop of ether in her ear and it will itch a little bit. She'll scratch, and each time she does, you put her in a bigger collar, until it finally slips off."

We wanted to show her sneaking out of the room by going through the transom. How did we do it? We had ten cats, and this one was the jumper. We had the trainer put his hand, holding meat, through the transom, and kept her hungry. She stared at his hand, and when we wanted to do a take we put a canary in a covered cage up there and started the cameras. We uncovered the cage, and, as the canary began to sing, we fired a gun. That cat took off like you've never seen — from the floor to a chair to the dresser and clear on up to the transom. We cut outside to the hall and she came down and ran like hell.

We ran the cat down New York streets and across the Brooklyn Bridge until she finally got to Ebbets Field. Ebbets Field had a high wall on which we put a lot of ivy, so you couldn't see the trainer's hand holding meat. The cat grabbed for the meat, slipped, jumped again, and finally got to the top of the wall, where she lay down, panting. Then she ran clear across the field, the players rubbed her head, and they won the game. Dogs are easy to work with — you can teach them and they will do the trick anywhere. Cats are difficult.

ATKINS: Was any of the picture shot in the east?

JACOBSON: We had a couple of the boys shoot the background for the Brooklyn Bridge. The baseball long shots were stock, and the rest we did on a field out here.

ATKINS: How did it feel to be back at Paramount after so many years? Was it very different from when you left?

JACOBSON: No. The only difference was that Mr. Freeman was more cordial to me.

ATKINS: How about *Aaron Slick from Punkin Crick*?

JACOBSON: The reason the picture was made was political. Frank Freeman was *it*, and Mrs. Freeman was a devout Southerner and a religious woman. For years, the play had been done in her church and in various southern churches, and it was her dream for *Aaron Slick* to be made into a movie. Her husband had tried to talk many producers into doing it, but nobody would touch it with a ten-foot pole.

Perlberg wanted to get his feet well entrenched at Paramount, so he started casting and lined up Alan Young and Dinah Shore. Just before we started, he went to New York and heard Robert Merrill, the opera singer.

He was a wonderful guy with a great voice, but he had no more business in that picture than the man in the moon.

I went to George after the third day's rushes and said, "We're making a terrible mistake You ought to stop the picture right now and recast this part."

What's more, Dinah sang on and on, and, as good as Dinah is, how much of her can you take in one sitting? Claude Binyon wrote a funny script and also directed, but it wasn't a funny picture. It died, and it almost ruined Dinah Shore.

When we did *Somebody Loves Me,* Perlberg did the same thing with Ralph Meeker. Ralph had never sung a note in his life, never danced a step, and here he was, playing Benny Fields, a vaudevillian, who did all kinds of things with a walking stick and an opera hat. To see poor Charlie O'Curran, the choreographer, try to whip this guy into shape was pathetic.

ATKINS: I think that was the only movie Irving Brecher directed.

JACOBSON: Irving Brecher did that one because he was very ambitious and he was a good friend of Perlberg's. Brecher was a very funny man, very caustic and sarcastic. Perlberg said, "Irving, if you write a good script, I'll let you direct it." That burned me, because I wanted to direct, but he did write a good script.

He had to deal with a meshugener named Betty Hutton. She didn't like him from the day she met him. There was a personality clash because Irving could be so sarcastic. She wouldn't talk or listen to him, so I wound up as the go-between on the set. She'd say, "Find out what he wants."

He'd say, "Tell her I want so and so." It was ridiculous, but that was the way we had to make it.

Betty Hutton was queen of all she surveyed. If she wanted the set at forty degrees, it was at forty degrees, because she said she couldn't get her verve up if the set were hot. On that picture, I was not the assistant director, so I was not around the set very much. On the third day, she called me to her dressing room on the set and said, "Can I ask you what you do around here? I see you around all day, but you don't do anything."

I said, "That's right."

"Do you work here?"

"Yes, I work for Perlberg-Seaton."

She said, "Exactly what do you do?"

I said, "I'm an ass-kisser, Miss Hutton. I'll show you exactly what I mean. Turn around and bend down." She did and I kissed her. That's the kind of humor she understood and from then on we were friends.

Eventually, it got to the point between her and Brecher where we were really losing time. After letting Betty know I was doing it, I went to Perlberg and told him to do something about it. He called a meeting with Irving, George, Charlie O'Curran — who was having trouble with her with the dance numbers — and me. Perlberg said to me, "Go between them and straighten it out."

I said, "No," and I'm glad I did.

Perlberg had it out with Betty, and she agreed to go back to work and try to get along with Brecher.

The day after they finished the picture Irving and Betty got married. It was crazy!

Later, when we were in Paris on *Little Boy Lost*, Barney Balaben came into our office and said, "We finally fired Betty Hutton. She had gone to Frank Freeman and insisted that she would not make her next picture unless her husband directed it. That meant she had broken her contract, so they fired her. From that moment on, Betty hit the skids, and Irving Brecher never directed another picture. He wrote a lot of scripts, and he made a fortune with *Life of Riley*. We got along fine, although I usually don't get along with a man like that — his tongue could cut you to ribbons.

ATKINS: We almost passed over *Anything Can Happen.*

JACOBSON: I think it was one of the best pictures we made. It was based on a book by the Pashvilys. Jose Ferrer did a superb job. He was suspected of Communism, and Paramount, especially Y. Frank Freeman, wasn't about to invest in a picture unless it was clean. Before the picture started, they went through everything in Washington, D.C., and he came out clean as a whistle, smelling like a rose.

But the damage had been done. They gave the picture a great send-off — a big publicity campaign proving he was clean and all kinds of previews. It got good reviews, and they kept it running week after week, hoping against hope, but the picture just died on the vine. I don't think they made ten dollars.

ATKINS: Did you find any other instance of the effects of the blacklist, in any of the films we've talked about?

JACOBSON: No. Only with Jose Ferrer. On *Anything Can Happen,* there was a slight row with Kim Hunter that had nothing to do with any of that. When she came out here, Perlberg wanted her to cut her hair shorter, but she refused. He threatened to recast, and she cut her hair.

ATKINS: There were some strong wills in the movie business.

JACOBSON: Mr. Perlberg was strong, believe me. You notice when I talk about him I refer to him as Mr. Perlberg. He could bully his way through if he had to, but he always had the head of the studio behind him.

He had been an agent in New York, I think with the William Morris office. He came out here and became a casting director at Columbia. He became second in command to Harry Cohn, because he could talk Harry Cohn's language.

They had a script which they couldn't lick, and Perlberg was going to produce it. After they'd tried about eight writers, somebody said, "There's a junior writer that MGM just brought out, George Seaton."

He'd worked on a Marx Brothers picture. They borrowed George from MGM, and he licked the script. Perlberg fell in love with him, and made arrangements for him to sign a contract with Columbia. From then on, George was Bill's boy — his writer.

Bill had an offer from Zanuck to come over and be second in command at Fox, but Bill couldn't accept because he was under contract to Harry Cohn. Before midnight on the expiration date of Bill's contract, he was supposed to receive a registered letter continuing the contract, but somebody in the Columbia legal department slipped up. He waited twenty-four hours, and then went to Zanuck and said, "I'm your boy, starting tomorrow morning."

Harry Cohn nearly had a heart attack. He tried to sue Bill, but there was nothing he could do. I don't think there was much love lost between Perlberg and Cohn. Of course, Bill took George Seaton with him.

ATKINS: I have met Perlberg and Seaton a few times, separately, and they seemed — .

JACOBSON: As far apart as two poles. I have answered the question at least two hundred times — how could those two men have gotten together and lasted? And, above all, how could I have lasted between them?

I had been an assistant director for so long that I had become a diplomat. George and I leaned over backwards towards Bill. For instance, when we went to Paris in 1952 for *Little Boy Lost,* Bill wanted to live at the Lancaster, which was *the* hotel — Zanuck had lived there. George, by the same token, wanted to live at a famous hotel across town. Where was I to be? Perlberg decided that my wife and I were to be in the room right next to his. His wife went to New York, he got sick, and my wife gave him chicken soup and took care of him. He liked to be babied.

He was a very immaculate man, very classy. He died a miserable death after open-heart surgery.

His wife recently married Jimmy Van Heusen. By the way, she and her two sisters were singers, before the Andrews Sisters. They were called the Brock Sisters. One of them married the famous trumpet player, Henry Busse. The Perlbergs had a son who became my assistant, so I had him in my hair all the time.

ATKINS: Did you, Mr. Perlberg, and Mr. Seaton have a definite agreement, about what you were to do?

JACOBSON: I was to be their major-domo, which meant that I was to do anything that came along. Any detail that Perlberg or George had to deal with, they could forget. I did it and brought them the results. If I needed their help I said, "This is where I am. From this point on I need your backing." Here is an example. In 1953, we made a picture called *The Bridges of Toko-Ri.* Mark Robson was the director. Francisco "Chico" Day was the assistant director. Bill Perlberg could not go on location because he was busy on post-production of another picture, and George Seaton couldn't go because he was writing *The Country Girl.* I went, and functioned as a producer. I was on the set all the time.

We were going to be out for nineteen days on the aircraft carrier, and we were going to use the flight deck as our movie sound stage, provided we didn't interfere with the operation of the ship. However, no matter what we had arranged in Washington, San Francisco, Tokyo or anywhere else, the captain of the ship had the last word.

Before we went to Japan we went to the aircraft carrier base in Oakland, and saw the twin catapults on the carrier. They were pretty exciting, and Bill Perlberg fell in love with them. The last thing Bill said to me was to be sure and bring back footage of them, no matter what.

On the second day out, the executive officer came to me and said, "I've got bad news for you. We only have one catapult operating, and we won't have the other repaired until we get back to port."

I said, "You can't do this," which they thought was very funny. I said, "I have to come back to Hollywood with twin catapult film or else I'll have to spend the rest of my life in Japan." I even asked if they could turn the ship around and go back and have it fixed. Of course, they said there was nothing that could be done.

The carrier was part of the Seventh Task Force, which was comprised of nineteen ships. Two aircraft carriers and a cruiser were in the center, ringed by the other ships.

Admiral Dave Johnson, a real southern gentleman who was in charge of the entire operation, invited us all to lunch on the other aircraft carrier, the Kearsage. We had to put on ties and white shirts, fly over in helicopters, and appear at the admiral's table. There was gleaming silverware, everyone was in white, and it was beautiful. Mickey Rooney, Bill Holden and Earl Holliman were there, and we were all seated according to protocol — it was very stiff.

I was always a little apprehensive about what people like Mickey Rooney would do or say at these little functions — who knows what Mickey would ever do? We had gone through six months of Washington, San Diego, and Tokyo. Now here we were at the lunch table with the admiral. This was his last hitch. He was going to go to Hawaii and be in charge of Military Air Transport Service. He was very pleased that we were aboard because it relieved the boredom. He was impressed by the actors. He was interested in what we were doing and said he would like to be with us while we were shooting. We said that would be fine. Then he said, "Well, gentlemen, as long as there are no ladies present, and you people are from Hollywood, let's break the ice and I'll tell a funny story. There was a man and woman and they were fornicating."

There was a silence. Mickey Rooney said, "Admiral, don't you mean — " and then he said the real word.

There was more silence. It hung there. All of a sudden the admiral threw his head back and started to laugh. Everybody started to laugh, thank God! I picked myself up from under the table, got back in my chair, looked at Rooney and said, "I was going to kill you, but thank you." From there on, it was smooth as silk.

When lunch was over we were so warm with each other that the admiral said, "Any complaints about the food?"

I said, "Of course not. The food was delicious."

We had the most wonderful guy, an assistant director named Chico Day, a Mexican American. He said, "Wait a minute. I've got a complaint. I don't know if you know it or not, but my name is Chico Alonzo Francisco Day, and I'm a Mexican. No frijoles, no enchiladas. What kind of a lunch is this?"

That got a big laugh, but about nine days later we were invited to lunch again. I don't know where they got it from, but we had a complete Mexican lunch.

We were sitting in the Sea of Japan, right off Korea, without twin catapults. After we had the first lunch on the Kearsage, the admiral said to me, "Send all your people back and stay here. I'd like to show you the ship."

I had seen the ship, or rather the sister ship, until it was coming out of my ears. While we walked around the ship he gave me his cap to wear. It was full of fruit salad and everybody was saluting me. It was great fun. We went up on the bridge. He let me sit in his chair and I watched how they did twin catapulting. All of a sudden I realized that this was a different ship, but who knew it? The only difference was that at certain points on the ship there was a number. The Kearsage was Number 34, while we were Number 33. Unfortunately, we had painted numbers on our ship's planes, because the only way the audience could recognize the actors was by those numbers, or by the name on the helmet.

After explaining our problem, I asked the admiral if we could shoot the planes taking off on his ship. He said, "Of course. Just give us a few hours' notice."

Then I told him that the 3 on the deck would have to be made a 4.

He said, "You guys are hotshots from Hollywood. We do things here in the Navy, too." He picked up the telephone, made a call, and said, "Watch."

Like that, a tiny jeep came out, two guys jumped out with paint brushes and paint, and made the 3 a 4. I said that was great, but that the 3 was dirty and aged, and the 4 looked brand new. He gave another order, and the jeep ran back and forth over the new number.

I was in on the transferring of the ten specially marked planes from our ship to the Kearsage, so that the audience would see them taking off. The planes had to rendezvous in the air and then land on the proper deck. It took an awful lot of notifying so that planes wouldn't jam into each other. That's an example of what I did.

ATKINS: At one time there were certain things that could not be photographed.

JACOBSON: This was 1953, and we didn't run into any of that.

There was one thing — sixteen of us went on location, and it took over six months to clear us. They went way back to your great-grandparents, to see where the family came from and so forth. The results were that fifteen men were absolutely clear. The other one, a cameraman, was a reformed alcoholic. As far as the Navy was concerned, it was all right, but they did want the studio to know that we were working on what they called "floating arsenals," and that it didn't take much of a mistake for them to go sky high.

We talked about it at great length, and okayed it. The cameraman never knew about it to this day, and we had no problems.

Many times, if Mark Robson was busy, I was the second unit director. When we got back to California, we needed a lot of airplane stuff. Bill Perlberg said that I could do it. I said I would on one condition: that Charlie Clarke be my cameraman, with Paul Mantz.

ATKINS: Where was this footage shot?

JACOBSON: On what I call the ass-end of Catalina. It looked like Korea. We also did a lot at an Air Force base near San Diego. The stuff we shot in Japan, which was supposed to be with Grace Kelly, was done with a double. Fredric March didn't go to Japan, either.

ATKINS: Between pictures with Perlberg and Seaton, were you still working?

JACOBSON: Well, there really never was a time between pictures. I was under contract to them, not to Paramount. One of the terms of their contract with Paramount was that their staff would include one person who was to be paid so much per week. There were no assistant producers who did what I did, and the only reason I was called assistant producer was because I was assistant to the two men. I did so many different jobs.

ATKINS: You worked on several films with Bing Crosby. How did you get along with him?

JACOBSON: Beautifully. I knew Bing before I worked with him. You see, in those days at the studio, you didn't have to work together to know each other — you met in the commissary, at the lunch table. I knew Dixie, his wife, very well. I worked with her, and he'd come over on the set. Once I got to work with Bing, in pictures like *Sing You Sinners* (1938), *Little Boy Lost* (1952), and *The Country Girl* (1954), I fell in love with the guy. I still have his golf book that he sent me. I can go on all afternoon and tell you about the virtues of Bing Crosby. He was a wonderful guy, but he had to like you. He wasn't the easiest guy in the world to get to know.

ATKINS: How about during the shooting of a movie?

JACOBSON: He was easy-going. The only thing he did do, was that one time he came to me and said, "I have a golf date. I didn't expect this date, because I never let anything interfere, but I have to do this, and I'm leaving at noon."

I said, "But you're in every scene today."

He said, "You go down to the office right now, and tell them what's happening. If you find other work to do, that's your business. But I want you to tell them it's me, not you that's responsible." That's the kind of a guy he was.

We had a wonderful time in Paris when we made *Little Boy Lost.* He and I practically lived together.

While we were in Paris, we hired a French unit manager and French assistant director. We had to find a child for the title part — a real French kid, with a real French accent. We wanted him to be skinny, emaciated, with eyes that would make you melt. We sent word out through our French connections at Paramount. We had a casting session, and we looked at all kinds of children. One kid walked in with a little make-up kit. He said the only English he knew: "I am Christian Fourcade, artiste."

We said, "Do you speak any English at all?"

He looked over to somebody, and they repeated it. He said in French, "I learn." Then he opened his make-up case, and inside it said, "Christian Fourcade, cinema artiste par excellence."

He was nine years old. We took him to George and he said, "We're in. We'll teach English to him even if we have to do it phonetically and put blackboards up."

We never saw his parents; they never came near us. He clung to me like a leech. He had read the book in French, and he started to learn the words of the script, and he learned a few American dirty words.

In the movie, he was supposed to live at an orphanage, so we went to an orphanage, bought all the clothes right off the backs of the orphans, and replaced those clothes with brand new ones. We had all the clothes cleaned, but they were still ragged. Christian Fourcade wasn't satisfied with the clothes. He and George got along well, and George wasn't satisfied with the clothes, either. One day Christian came in completely dressed as Little Boy Lost. There he was. You couldn't have done better if you had Edith Head design it. "Where did he get it?" Every time he went home he looked at children. If he liked something, like a sweater, he'd go to the child and buy the sweater. He took a kid into a shoe store, bought him a pair of shoes, and took the old ones.

Christian could also sing and dance. He was a Mickey Rooney and Donald O'Connor rolled into one, except that he had Margaret O'Brien's eyes, or Peggy Ann Garner's in *Jane Eyre.*

Bing had been in England, and came to Paris to meet Christian and they fell in love with each other. Bing was his idol, long before the picture. He had all of Bing's records, and Bing taught him a few boo-boo-boo-boos.

When we came back here Bing put him on his radio show and he stole it. They were making a picture at

Paramount called *Red Garters,* which Rosemary Clooney was in. She sang like a bird and had a figure like nobody's business. This child fell head over heels in love with Rosemary, like only a Frenchman can, at ten years old. I don't think she realized how deep it was, and nothing ever came of it, of course.

The thing that shows George's perception was the casting of the laundress for *Little Boy Lost.* In his mind's eye he would have liked to have had a short dumpy woman. One afternoon he said, "I want you to go with me tonight to a lesbian joint, before I talk to Bill about it."

The mistress of ceremonies was about five foot one — up and down, high and wide, with red hair like you've never seen. George had her hair dyed black and streaked with gray. He put a sweater and other clothes on her and she became the laundress.

She had a couple of Great Danes. One day it was raining and we couldn't shoot, so we were having lunch in the hotel dining room. At the doorway of the dining room was a big table with a display of pastries. She swept into the room with the dogs, and their big tails swept all the whipped cream off of the pastries.

Bing received the letter about his wife Dixie's condition, just before he did a beautiful scene in the picture. I know that's what he was thinking of while he was doing it. Right after it was shot, he was on a plane back to Los Angeles. She died within a week or so.

I don't know if I can explain what close friends Seaton and I were. I think we had lunch together every day of the week, because we had things to talk about alone. I could always tell if George had something really private. He'd get a little table in the corner and let Perlberg go someplace else.

One day I knew there was something up, and I asked what it was. He said, "I have an idea about *The Country Girl.* For the drunken husband I would like Bing Crosby.

Forget the Bing Crosby that you know. Visualize Bing Crosby playing Frank."

I said, "What? Bing Crosby plays a drunk, a has-been?"

He said, "You said that same thing about Grace Kelly playing a dowdy old woman. Do me a favor. Go in and talk to him, and tell him what you think."

I said, "Now that I think of it, I think he'd be great." He said, "I have a problem. I don't know Bing and you know him very, very well. Perlberg knows him better than you, but he doesn't really know him. I don't want Bing to think Perlberg wants him. Will you break the ice to him? First ask him if he read the book, and have the script in your hand."

Bill Perlberg's and Bing's relationship was not like mine. I was the kind of guy who could walk in, kick my shoes off and sit in his dressing room all afternoon without a drink. We were good friends. So I went and talked to Bing, and he said, "Oh, no." He was scared to death to do the part.

But I got him to read the script. I said, "You have the greatest opportunity that you've ever had in your life. Can you do anything except sing and dance?"

He said, "What about *Little Boy Lost*?"

I said, "That was pretty good, but now there's a better idea, *The Country Girl*."

He said, "You're out of your mind."

I said, "Well, then George Seaton's out of his mind. I'm here because he sent me, because he doesn't know you."

George came in, and finally, Bing said he would do it, but he said, "How am I going to play this guy? You know, my hairpieces and all that."

George said, "I have a wonderful idea for a scene about your hairpieces. In one of the scenes you'll be sitting at the dressing room table, just after you come offstage, and I want you to take the hairpieces off, right in the scene."

Bing said, "With my following? The fans? I'll get killed." He thought for a while, and suddenly he said, "Look, George, anything you want me to do, I'll do. I'm scared to death, but if you feel I can do it — how does Bill feel about it?"

George said, "Fine, fine."

Bing played it and did a very good job. Grace Kelly and Bill Holden were great in that picture, too.

ATKINS: You had worked with Bing Crosby many years before that. Did you find that he changed over the years?

JACOBSON: No. From the day I met him, he was the same Bing all the time. If you didn't know him, you'd call him cold. You couldn't get to him. Either you were a very close friend and you were within him, or you weren't. When we were doing *Sing You Sinners* he was almost bashful. He didn't want people patting him on the back.

He was a wonderful guy, and I have nothing but good things to say about him.

Moving Around

ATKINS: I think *The Country Girl* is the last picture you did with Perlberg and Seaton at Paramount. Was there any special reason why you left?

JACOBSON: Yes. I was seduced. The head of a beer company fell in love with a dear friend of ours, Linda Darnell, and they used her for advertising Rheingold Beer. This was after she was divorced from Pev Marley. When the photographers came to her house to make color stills for advertising, Phillip Liebman, the president of Rheingold, came along. He badgered her for a date, but she wouldn't go on a date with him because he wasn't the most attractive guy. Okay, she would go on a date with him if my wife and I went along. That night we went to the Villa Nova, on Sunset Boulevard. I made with the jokes and he laughed.

He invited us to go to Europe for Queen Elizabeth's coronation and paid all our expenses. Linda was in Italy and met us in England. The company gave me as much time off as I needed.

All of a sudden, Rheingold came up with an offer for a three-year job for me, at double the money I was getting. I would travel all over the world with Douglas Fairbanks, Jr., making the *Rheingold Theatre*. All I had to do was watch over the pictures so that when they were shown in New York City, the customers could understand what the British actors were saying.

I went to George and said, "I love working with you, but is it possible for you to match what I can get from this offer?"

I explained that Gloria and I would be traveling at their expense, too. I said, "I'd rather stay with you."

He said, "We can't. I can't go to Paramount and ask them to double your salary. But why don't you do the three years with Rheingold, and then come back to us."

I went to Europe. After the three years which were set, we made a deal where I worked from week to week. This was for the anthology show, *Douglas Fairbanks Presents.*

Douglas had a studio in Boreham Wood, outside of London. Each year we made eight shows in Germany, mostly in Bavaria, eight in Italy, and a few in Greece. We had a ball.

ATKINS: What was your official capacity in this company?

JACOBSON: I worked with Douglas. I was overseeing the thing, and protecting the interests of the sponsor, who paid for half the cost. For the first few weeks it was a little tough because the people in his company did not know I was a motion picture man. They thought I was an advertising agency man. Douglas knew it because I had been a second cameraman on one of his first pictures, *Stella Dallas,* when he was sixteen years old. He and I got along fine.

One day he called me in and said, "You're disrupting my whole organization because you won't okay this and that."

I said, "You're a perfectionist. Do you want that junk on the screen? These pictures are made primarily for New York City, and people will laugh at them."

He didn't like doing the show. His friends were calling him a beer salesman. But he needed the money.

Most of the crew were Canadian. We had casting directors who were lazy. They had to go out at night and find people, in nightclubs and other places. I did all kinds of jobs, without stepping on other people's toes.

ATKINS: Did you live in Europe, or were you commuting?

JACOBSON: I was commuting. The first time I was gone, I was away for eleven months. If I had been smart I would have lived there, because after eighteen months I wouldn't have had to pay taxes.

At the end of the four-and-a-half years they decided not to make any more. Phillip Liebman and I sat at the Beverly Hills Hotel pool. He said, "We're going to give you more money, and we're going to make a whole new department. We're going to put you in charge of all television pertaining to Rheingold Beer. We're not going to make any pictures, we're going to buy them. You'll have an office with Foote, Cone, and Belding, on Park Avenue, and it will be your job to buy shows. We will arrange an apartment for you, but there's one thing you'll have to do — you'll have to live in New York."

I said, "I just blew a hell of a good job. You don't have enough money to make me live in New York." He tried to persuade me, but I refused, and we called the whole thing off.

ATKINS: Next, you were at Twentieth Century-Fox.

JACOBSON: Yes, working for Jerry Wald. That lasted until the actors' strike.

ATKINS: Was this the same kind of a job that you had with Seaton and Perlberg?

JACOBSON: No. It came about because Jerry needed somebody. He was having lunch with Mark Robson, and Mark recommended me. I can't describe what it was, except that the fact that I was there made him very comfortable. I had no title with Jerry. I had no screen credit. We were going to prove my job with him first, and then I would become associate producer. The reason I wanted to go with him was that I'd have a chance to either produce or direct.

He was a fascinating man to watch operate. He had been a writer, a newspaper man. A big star would come in to discuss something, and the star would say, "Jerry, it's not for me."

If Jerry wanted this star, he'd say, "All right. It's not for you. But boy, I've got another one. I've got it right in my pocket. Listen to this." He'd reach in his pocket as if it were there and make up a story as he sat there. I saw this happen many times. He was one of the great con artists of all time, but he delivered.

ATKINS: Did you sit in on a lot of those conferences?

JACOBSON: Yes, yes. He had his own company. He had his own bungalow with six offices. I had an office by myself. Anybody he wanted, he hired. He had first dibs on whoever was under contract at the studio. If he wanted somebody special he got them. He didn't have to go to anyone. He had nothing to do with Zanuck. Jerry's wife ran an awful lot of it, also. She had great influence over him.

The one person that did not get along with him, and whom he didn't like, was Harry Brand. He didn't need Harry Brand, because he had his own publicity department, and many times he sent things out that Harry Brand knew nothing about.

There was an awful lot of detail that he didn't want anything to do with, and I handled it. There were unpleasant things also, like when Edmund Goulding, a fine director, had fallen on bad times. Jerry would call me and say, "Look, Eddie is coming over here, and I don't have a picture for him. Do something about it."

I had to shoulder that, and it was a pretty sad job, until Eddie finally realized that Jerry didn't want to see him. He was finished.

ATKINS: Which of the Jerry Wald films were you involved in?

JACOBSON: I directed the second unit on *The Story of Page One,* for which we had some scenes to make between Gig Young and Rita Hayworth in the basement of the jail downtown.

Jerry said, "Get somebody to direct it."

I said, "I'll do it," and he said, "Fine."

There were many things Clifford Odets needed and wanted to know about and I was able to explain them to him. There were an awful lot of things those writers from Broadway could not grasp.

ATKINS: *The Story of Page One* may be the only film Clifford Odets directed.

JACOBSON: He had also directed *None but the Lonely Heart* in 1944.

ATKINS: Did you work on *Let's Make Love* in 1959?

JACOBSON: Yes, but there was nothing much you could do. Cukor, God bless him, didn't need any help. The only way I could help a little bit was through Whitey Snyder, Marilyn Monroe's make-up man. She trusted him. He and I were very good friends.

He came to me, because they were having trouble. She didn't like something she had seen in the rushes, and he asked me to go to her and tell her that the rushes looked all right. He said that she would remember me from years ago at Fox. I went to her, and she looked at me with the most unbelieving eyes.

She said, "You must be kidding me. What do you need?"

I said, "Marilyn, I'm not kidding. I'm telling you the truth."

I couldn't convince her. Whitey Snyder was about the only individual alive that she ever believed. Other than that I had nothing much to do with *Let's Make Love.*

ATKINS: Did you work with Henry King on *Beloved Infidel*?

JACOBSON: It was the same thing with that. Henry King didn't need anybody.

ATKINS: What about *Sons and Lovers*?

JACOBSON: That was made strictly in England. That script was all set before I ever got there. You couldn't do much with Don Siegel. He's his own man. So those are the only pictures, and all I did was a job.

ATKINS: Then I think you went back to Paramount, with Mel Shavelson in 1961.

JACOBSON: The way that happened was that I went to have lunch at Paramount one day, and it happened that the assistant director on *On the Double,* a Danny Kaye picture, was needed for a picture they were going to make in Japan. They asked me to take over in his place. I hit it off with Mel, and we had a wonderful time.

ATKINS: How did you like working with Danny Kaye?

JACOBSON: I loved him. I was just crazy about working with him. He's such a decent, nice man. I had no trouble working with anybody I respected, especially when I respected their talent. For me, he's Mr. Talent. This man can do anything to perfection.

I did another one with Mel, *A New Kind of Love,* with Paul Newman and Joanne Woodward. It had a wonderful cast including Eva Gabor. That was also done at Paramount.

ATKINS: Mel Shavelson was another director who had been a writer.

JACOBSON: He still is and always will be. He's a brilliant man. Then after that they called me to go to MGM to work out some weeks that were left on *Mutiny on the Bounty.* They came back from Tahiti, and the assistant director was stuck down there. I did about eight weeks with Milestone. While I was at MGM I worked on *The Impossible Years.* In between they threw me onto a television series, called *Jericho.*

ATKINS: Who was in that series?

JACOBSON: Complete unknowns. It lasted one season.

ATKINS: What can you tell me about *Camelot,* which you worked on a few years later?

JACOBSON: I was at home. I was beginning to have trouble with my hips, not too bad, but if I stayed on my feet too long I started to get a lot of pain. My wife was very, very ill, and had been for years. I was more or less retired, so that I could be with her. I was sitting at home bewailing my fate because the Guild money had become very good, and damn it, I wasn't getting any of it, after I had worked for all of those years.

My phone rang, and it was Joel Freeman. I had known Joel at MGM. He was Dore Schary's nephew, had gone to Warner Bros., and at this point was assistant to Mr. Warner himself. Mr. Warner was making his last picture. He had decided not to make *Camelot* until he went to England, saw it on the stage, and fell in love with the production designer. He said, "If that man will come to Hollywood and design the production of *Camelot*, I'll make the picture."

The designer did come to Hollywood. Although they had art directors, he designed the sets, and he designed the costumes as well.

Joshua Logan went to Spain to do the long opening shots. The first thing he did when he came back was to say to Joel Freeman, "You have to get me a different assistant. This man has no enthusiasm. I need the kind of man who, even if he's not telling the truth, at the end of a scene will slap me on the back and say, 'Hey!' But this guy is so — I get nothing from him, and I feel I haven't done a good job. I cannot go on with the picture with this man." Joel snapped his fingers and said, "I know exactly the guy for you."

That's when he called me and said, "Will you come in and see me?"

I said, "What's it all about?" I went to the studio and had lunch with him, and he told me the whole story. He said, "You can do it. The only person you have to pass is Josh Logan."

I said, "I saw *South Pacific* on Broadway. I think he's the greatest director. It would be a great pleasure to work with him."

He said, "You may change your mind about that. He's a little bit eccentric."

I said, "So what? I've worked with eccentric people before."

He said, "You have to pass him."

We went over to Logan's office, where you sank into the carpets. He was way down at the other end of the office. He stood up, came around, and shook hands with me. I said, "What a pleasure, what an opportunity to work with the man who did *South Pacific*."

He immediately wanted me to work with him.

Joel said that everything was all set, but I said, "Does anybody around here want to talk money?"

I told him what I wanted, and Joel said, "I don't think I have the authority to give you that kind of money. I'll have to go see J. L." He went out of the room, and was back in five minutes.

I said, "Joel, you didn't go to see J. L., did you?"

He said, "No."

I said, "You had the authority to give me what I asked before you ever left this office, but you thought I'd change my mind and call you back." They gave me the money that I asked for.

There was something like four weeks between the time Logan came back and the time he picked up production. During those four weeks they pre-recorded Richard Harris and Vanessa Redgrave performing the music.

Now we started to make the picture. We didn't have much trouble during the recordings, because Al Newman took that over. When Al Newman takes things over, Al Newman takes things over. But I noticed that there was all kinds of unhappiness between Richard Harris and Logan.

Vanessa came over, and I showed her her dressing room. She cried. One day I said to her, "Did you ever hear of ginger wine?"

She said, "Sure."

I said, "When I was in London, I used to buy it. I can't find it anywhere." Two weeks later she came in with a bottle of ginger wine. A friend of hers had sent it to her, for me. So that's the way I started with Vanessa — fine.

Then we started to shoot the picture. I knew he had made movies before, but I discovered that Josh Logan didn't know his ass from a hole in the ground about making movies. He had made *Picnic*, and he had damn near ruined *South Pacific*. He was completely mixed up. He never knew where the hell he was going, and I told Joel after the first ten days.

He said, "I know. That's why I wanted you here. Try to keep him on an even keel."

I'd say to him, "Look, Josh —." I never called him Josh. I called him Mr. Logan. "Look, right now, let's quit shooting for the day, and devote the rest of the day to lining up tomorrow morning's shot. We need a good start in the morning. It keeps you going."

He'd say, "Fine. Wonderful idea."

Everything I said was "wonderful idea," until I said to myself, I can't be that wonderful. Sure enough, the next morning he'd come in and say, "All right, boys."

We'd say, "Want to dry run it, Mr. Logan?"

He'd say, "No, wait a minute," and he'd make a change. The change would take an hour-and-a-half.

He'd say, "Well, I only want to move the camera that much."

I'd say to Dick Kline, the cameraman, "Tell him, Dick. When you move the camera that much you have to change the lighting."

I stopped arguing with him. What the hell.

Well, this went on, and then he and Richard Harris got into fights like you have never seen or heard. We used to see to it that the kids who brought visitors around would bypass our set. The language was filthy and foul. Logan was the strongest guy in the world. He could have broken my back.

Then Vanessa started to show her true colors. I got along great with Richard Harris, but Vanessa and I tangled.

One day she came in and said, "Why do you call me at nine o'clock in the morning when I don't work until half past ten?"

I said, "It just happened that when we got in this morning Mr. Logan —."

She said, "Don't blame it on Mr. Logan."

I said, "I'm not blaming anybody. I'm telling you facts."

She said, "I'm not coming in from now on."

I said, "Don't come in. I'll go get Mr. Freeman and we'll get another assistant director put on just to serve you."

I said a few more things to her. From that moment on we never said a word to each other. My assistants did it. I wouldn't even talk to her. Richard Harris said, "You were very naughty to Vanessa."

I said, "Oh, she put you up to this."

A few days later he was doing a scene and she walked up to him and said, "Richard, don't you think — "

He said, "Oh, the day I have to take acting lessons from you!"

In the middle of all the turmoil was Logan. He wasn't getting along with Vanessa or Richard Harris. We had about another month to go. It was a long picture, and this was the end, the last reel.

One day I went to find out what was holding Harris up. He had an entrance through the big doors. While I was back there I heard this voice, "Artie!"

It was Logan. He said, "What's going on there? Can't you get organized?"

Well, my hair stood right straight up on end. I lost my temper completely. I came running right up in front of him, and practically screamed in his nose. I said, "Don't you ever say that word to me again. Why, for

Christ's sakes, you don't know what time it is when it comes to the word organized. You've got this company so screwed up it's pathetic, and I keep it on an even keel for you, and you have the gall, the guts, to tell me to get organized? You can take this picture and stick it right up your ass, Mr. Logan."

He said, "You can't talk to me like that. You get off my set."

I said, "What? Your set? I've got some news for you. There's a man named Jack L. Warner, who owns this set. You work here the same as I do. Your job is to direct. Don't you order me off a set."

I called the second assistant over and said, "For safety with me and the Guild, so I don't leave a company high and dry —"

Then I said, "Joel, did you hear all this?"

He said, "Yes."

I said, "I'm through."

ATKINS: Were there a lot of people around?

JACOBSON: Oh, of course. A company can smell blood. I took my coat and said, "I'm through," and walked off.

The first thing Joel did was to call it a day. I started to drive off the lot when a cop stopped me and said that Joel wanted to see me in his office. I went there, and Joel said he understood the whole thing and had expected something like this to happen. He said that he would take the assistant off the Fred Astaire picture, *Finian's Rainbow,* and put me on that, but that my salary would still be charged to *Camelot*.

I said, "That's very decent of you, but I think that guy's nuts."

Joel said, "I know he's nuts. But we're stuck with him."

The next morning I was going to start working on *Finian's Rainbow*. At six o'clock my phone rang, at home. "Artie, this is Josh."

I said, "Josh who?"

He said, "Josh Logan. Remember, *Camelot*? What the hell happened yesterday afternoon?"

"Don't you know, Mr. Logan? What do you want?"

He said, "I want you to come back to work and let's get on with it." Then he apologized for what had happened. I could see dollar signs, I could see Joel Freeman, and it was not going to do me any good in the industry. When an assistant director loses his temper, it is not good for his reputation.

ATKINS: You mentioned something about the Guild.

JACOBSON: If there's going to be anything like that, you can't just walk off a picture. The least I could have done would have been to wait until the end of the day. Anyhow, the upshot of it was that I went to work.

As I drove through the gate, the cop held up his hand and said, "Mr. Logan came through here a half-hour ago, and he stopped here and told me that he had phoned you and apologized to you. He wanted me to know it, and he wanted me to stop you and tell you."

Between the gate and the set I must have been stopped twelve times, the same story. He had said, "I just apologized to Artie," to everybody that he knew on the way to the set. The same thing happened when I got to the set. He walked over to me and put his arm around my shoulder. I said, "Mr. Logan, take your arm off my shoulder. We have a job to do. I'll go ahead and do it, but it's completely impersonal." Away we went. When the picture was over, he sent me a little Excalibur, the sword, and he invited me to the party. I never saw him again until one day when I was at Paramount. I was having lunch at Oblath's. He came in, and you'd think I was his long-lost son.

Frank Caffey called me. I said to him, "I know what you want, but I don't want to do it. You want me to do *Paint Your Wagon,* because nobody else wants to work with him." Frank asked me to come over and talk to him, which I did. The money was fabulous.

I said, "It's bad enough to work with this guy on the stage, but to go to Oregon? The only good thing you've got is Frank Shaw, the unit manager. I don't want any part of it." He insisted that I had to do it, but I refused.

They put somebody else on it, and about two weeks after the picture was in production, Frank Shaw flew back and said to Paramount, "You've got to stop the picture, take this man off it, and put another director on."

They asked him who he'd suggest. He was Richard Brooks' man, and he tried to get Richard to drop what he was doing, and go up and take over *Paint Your Wagon.* He didn't, so they were stuck. They went back to the location twice, and Logan took so long that they ran out of snow. It was a shambles.

I was still lucid when they finished that picture, and that's the end of my story with Josh Logan. You never know what a person is like until you live with them or work with them.

Camelot was a picture loaded with closeups. I only saw the picture once, and that was the night that Jack Warner ran it for just a handful of us.

Later I saw it on television. It played in two parts, over a period of two weeks, and it was so chopped up I couldn't follow it. You couldn't tell what the hell it was, even with the beautiful music and everything. Al Newman did a magnificent job. They made a mistake to start with — this show called for magnificent voices. None of them had it.

ATKINS: I think you did *The Impossible Years* soon after this.

JACOBSON: Yes, it was a pleasurable picture. Michael Gordon was a nice guy to work with. The producer was a wonderful man, Larry Weingarten. I loved him. I loved working with David Niven. He was the salt of the earth. Everybody else in it was great. Michael Gordon had directed quite a few of those good comedies with Doris Day, and he had been a well-known stage director. The last thing I heard about Michael was that he had been a professor of cinema at UCLA, and they were mustering him out because he had passed the age of retirement. The State of California wouldn't allow him to work.

ATKINS: They've lost some good people that way.

JACOBSON: Well, USC picked up quite a few of them.

ATKINS: I think the only other picture I know that you worked on is *Zigzag* (1970).

JACOBSON: That was a routine picture. It was a good script, but it didn't come off.

ATKINS: Had Richard Colla come from television?

JACOBSON: Yes. He was under contract to Universal.

ATKINS: Did you notice any difference with directors who came from television — compared to those who'd started in films?

JACOBSON: Oh, yes. It was more difficult for me to work with the ones from television because they would okay so many things that I knew weren't okay. They weren't finished, and when you saw the picture put together you said, "What the hell difference does it make?"

There's only one other thing I didn't mention. During George Seaton's tenure as President of the Academy of Motion Picture Arts and Sciences, I assisted him on every one of the *Academy Awards Ceremony* shows. That was a big job, but it was great fun. We had Johnny Green in the pit all the time.

ATKINS: Would you have an official title for the Awards show?

JACOBSON: Yes. Assistant to the Producer.

ATKINS: Has the function of the assistant director changed in recent years?

JACOBSON: Yes, because they're working so fast, both in movies for television and theatres. Every once in a while I see a shooting schedule and it tells you what you are going to do from 11:00 a.m. until 11:10. The schedules were never laid out to the minute like that. A program picture that we used to make in thirty-six days is now made in twelve or fifteen. The laws they have today are crazy. If you go one second beyond eleven o'clock, the company suffers a meal penalty. You can't breathe.

A lot of the assistants are pretty noisy, and of course when I go on a set and I look at my own workers, they look dirty — with beards, long hair, and beads.

There's another thing I've noticed: when you go into some of the old studios, MGM, for instance, the stages smell bad — they're decaying. I don't really want to go on a set anymore.

The only thing I miss now, frankly, is the money, because the money has gone to astronomical amounts. I don't know how they are going to continue to make pictures with the kind of money they're paying everybody. The basic is at least a thousand dollars a week.

We went to a party one night, and a very dear friend of mine, a cameraman, started to encourage me, saying that if it wasn't for my hips I could do a job. By the time he got through, I was so drunk they had to carry me out to the car. The very thought of going back to work was wonderful. You see, I loved the work.

Filmography

1918-1923

Production Assistant

Million Dollar Dollies - Director: Ivan Abramson
Lest We Forget - Director: Leonce Perret
Moral Suicide - Director: Ivan Abramson
Three Miles Out - Director: Irvin Willat

Cameraman

The Federated Screen Revues (Shorts)

Third Assistant Cameraman

Zaza

Second Cameraman

The Scarecrow - Director: Frank Tuttle
Puritan Passions - Director: Frank Tuttle
Various comedy shorts - Director: Richard Thorpe

1924

Second Cameraman

Grit - Director: Frank Tuttle
Reckless Lady - Director: Howard Higgin

1925

Second Cameraman

Stella Dallas - Director: Henry King

1926

Assistant Director
The Dancer of Paris - Director: Al Santell

1927

First Assistant Director
Manpower - Director: Clarence Badger

Second Assistant Director
Afraid to Love - Director: Edward H. Griffith
Children of Divorce - Directors: Frank Lloyd and Josef von Sternberg
Gentlemen of Paris - Director: Harry D'Arrast

1928

Assistant Director
Sawdust Parade - Director: Luther Reed

First Assistant Director
Feel My Pulse - Director: Gregory La Cava

Second Assistant Director
Someone to Love - Director: F. Richard Jones

1929

First Assistant Director
The Saturday Night Kid - Director: Edward Sutherland
The Wild Party - Director: Dorothy Arzner
Chinatown Nights - Director: William A. Wellman
The Mysterious Dr. Fu Manchu - Director: Rowland V. Lee

1930

First Assistant Director
The Street of Chance - Director: John Cromwell
The Sea God - Director: George Abbott
Sea Legs - Director: Victor Heerman

1930 (cont.)

Honor Among Lovers - Director: Dorothy Arzner

Assistant Director

Paramount on Parade - various Directors

1931

First Assistant Director

The Royal Family of Broadway - Director: George Cukor
Kick In - Director: Richard Wallace
Rich Man's Folly - Director: John Cromwell

1932

First Assistant Director

Madame Butterfly - Director: Marion Gering
A Farewell to Arms - Director: Frank Borzage
The Devil and the Deep - Director: Marion Gering
If I Had a Million - Directors: Ernst Lubitsch, James Cruze, Norman McLeod, Norman Taurog, Stephen Roberts, William Seiter, H. Bruce Humberstone

1933

First Assistant Director

Too Much Harmony - Director: Edward Sutherland
An American Tragedy - Director: Josef von Sternberg
International House - Director: Edward Sutherland

1934

Co-Director

Wagon Wheels - Co-Director: Charles Barton

First Assistant Director

The Search for Beauty - Director: Erle C. Kenton
Shoot the Works - Director: Wesley Ruggles
Good Dame - Director: Marion Gering

1935

First Assistant Director

The Big Broadcast of 1936 - Director: Norman Taurog
The Bride Comes Home - Director: Wesley Ruggles

Director

Home on the Range

1936

First Assistant Director

F-Man - Director: Edward F. Cline

1937

First Assistant Director

I Met Him in Paris - Director: Wesley Ruggles
True Confession - Director: Wesley Ruggles

1938

First Assistant Director

Sing You Sinners - Director: Wesley Ruggles
Say It In French - Director: Andrew L. Stone

1939-1940

Head of Talent - Paramount Pictures

1941

First Assistant Director

I Wanted Wings - Director: Mitchell Leisen

1942

First Assistant Director

Sundown - Director: Henry Hathaway

Director of additional scenes

Thunderbirds - Director: William A. Wellman

1942 (cont.)

Assistant to Mark Sandrich, Producer-Director

The Hollywood Victory Caravan Tour

1943

First Assistant Director

Jane Eyre - Director: Robert Stevenson
Crash Dive - Director: Archie Mayo
Happy Land - Director: Irving Pichel

1944

First Assistant Director

Something for the Boys - Director: Lewis Seiler
The Purple Heart - Director: Lewis Milestone

1945

First Assistant Director

The Dolly Sisters - Director: Irving Cummings
Junior Miss - Director: George Seaton
Colonel Effingham's Raid - Director: Irving Pichel
Diamond Horseshoe - Director: George Seaton

1946

First Assistant Director

Smoky - Director: Louis King
Centennial Summer - Director: Otto Preminger

1947

First Assistant Director

Miracle on 34th Street - Director: George Seaton
The Shocking Miss Pilgrim - Director: George Seaton
Thunder in the Valley - Director: Louis King

1948

First Assistant Director

Apartment for Peggy - Director: George Seaton

1948 (cont.)

Give My Regards to Broadway - Director: Lloyd Bacon
The Big Lift - Director: George Seaton

1949

First Assistant Director

I Was a Male War Bride - Director: Howard Hawks
Chicken Every Sunday - Director: George Seaton
Mr. Belvedere Goes to College - Director: Elliott Nugent
The Walls of Jericho - Director: John M. Stahl

1950

First Assistant Director

For Heaven's Sake - Director: George Seaton
Love That Brute - Director: Alexander Hall
I'll Get By - Director: Richard Sale

1951

Assistant to the Producer and Second Unit Director

Rhubarb - Director: Arthur Lubin

1952

Assistant to the Producer

Aaron Slick from Punkin Crick - Director: Claude Binyon
Somebody Loves Me - Director: Irving Brecher

First Assistant Director

Anything Can Happen - Director: George Seaton

1953

First Assistant Director

Little Boy Lost - Director: George Seaton

1954

Assistant to the Producers and Second Unit Director
The Bridges of Toko-Ri - Director: George Seaton

Assistant to the Producers
The Country Girl - Director: George Seaton

1954-1957

Executive
The Rheingold Theatre (Television)

1955 -1957

Assistant to the Producer
Academy Awards Ceremony Shows,
Academy of Motion Picture Arts and Sciences

1958

Executive
Douglas Fairbanks Presents (Television)

1959

Assistant to the Producers
The Story of Page One - Director: Jerry Wald
Beloved Infidels - Director: Henry King

1960

Assistant to the Producers
Sons and Lovers - Director: Jack Cardiff
Let's Make Love - Director: George Cukor

1961

First Assistant Director
On the Double - Director: Melville Shavelson

1962

First Assistant Director (portions only)
Mutiny on the Bounty - Director: Lewis Milestone

1963

First Assistant Director
A New Kind of Love - Director: Melville Shavelson

1963-1964

First Assistant Director
Jericho (Television series)

1967

First Assistant Director
Camelot - Director: Joshua Logan

1968

First Assistant Director
The Impossible Years - Director: Michael Gordon

1970

First Assistant Director
Zigzag - Director: Richard Colla

Index

C

E

F

G

I

J

K

L

M

N

O

P

R

S

Y

Z